The Grandissimes
CENTENNIAL ESSAYS

The Grandissimes

CENTENNIAL ESSAYS

Thomas J. Richardson
EDITOR

UNIVERSITY PRESS OF MISSISSIPPI
Jackson
1981

*This volume is authorized and sponsored
by the
University of Southern Mississippi*

Library of Congress Cataloging in Publication Data

The Grandissimes: centennial essays.

(Southern quarterly series)
Essays originally published in the Southern
quarterly, v. 18, no. 4, summer 1980.
Includes bibliographical references and index.
1. Cable, George Washington, 1844-1925.
Grandissimes—Addresses, essays, lectures.
I. Richardson, Thomas J. II. Series
PS1244.G63G7   183'.4   81-13122
ISBN 0-87805-149-X   AACR2

Contents

Introduction:
Honoré Grandissime's Southern Dilemma

For Arlin Turner
(November 25, 1909–April 24, 1980)

This collection of essays marking the centennial of *The Grandissimes* (1880) is dedicated to the memory of Arlin Turner, whose *George W. Cable, A Biography* (Durham: Duke Univ. Press, 1956; Baton Rouge: Louisiana State Univ. Press, 1966) has been the basis for continuing scholarship on Cable and his work. In addition to publishing the biography and a number of critical essays on Cable, Professor Turner edited and made available many of Cable's original materials—letters, stories, essays, and speeches. Any contemporary scholar who studies *The Grandissimes* owes him a great debt.

If Mark Twain is not included, then Merrill Skagg's assertion that Cable was the most important Southern artist working in the late nineteenth century is quite correct.[1] *The Grandissimes* alone sets Cable apart from lesser writers of the Deep South who lived and wrote in the local color era after the Civil War, though one might add Cable's other early fiction about New Orleans, *Old Creole Days* (1879) and *Madame Delphine* (1881), or his courageous essays on civil rights, such as *The Silent South* (1885) or *The Negro Question* (1890), as significant contributions to American literary history. *The Grandissimes,* however, is primarily responsible for Cable's enduring reputation; since Turner's biography, it has received substantial critical attention from such distinguished scholars as Richard Chase, Louis D. Rubin, Jr., and Jay Martin, among others.[2] Much of the criticism has supported the significance and acknowledged the complexity of the novel. For example, Chase says that "in this novel about life in New Orleans in 1803 Cable transcended his usual limitations and wrote a

1

minor masterpiece," and "there are things in *The Grandissimes* that are beyond the reach of any of Cable's contemporaries."[3] For Rubin, "*The Grandissimes* may be said to be the first 'modern' Southern novel. . . . If the modern Southern novel has been characterized by its uncompromising attempt to deal honestly with the complexity of Southern racial experience, then *The Grandissimes* was the first important work of fiction written by a Southerner in which that intention is manifested."[4] In addition, *The Grandissimes* is "more than a disquisition on race; it [is] also the picture of a society in transition, very much a *Kulturroman* as his friend the novelist H. H. Boyesen had predicted."[5] Boyesen defines a *Kulturroman* as "a novel in which the struggling forces of opposing civilizations crystalize [sic] and in which they find their enduring monument."[6]

Indeed, by setting the novel in 1803 in New Orleans, immediately after the Louisiana Purchase, Cable was able to capture the conflict between the Creoles, the descendants of the original French and Spanish settlers, and the invading Americans whose government was newly in power. At the time of the novel's action, the Grandissimes are an important Creole family, grown numerous with complex, dark branches in the family tree. The Creole heritage is already a century deep, and the family takes great pride in tracing their lineage and traditions back to the first settlers. At the *bal masqué* in September 1803 which opens the novel, the white Honoré Grandissime, current leader of the family, is masked as Epaminondas Fusilier, the first of the Grandissimes, and his friend Charlie Keene is the ancestral bride, the Indian Queen Lufki-Humma.

Yet the power of the Grandissimes, like the rest of the Creoles, is already slightly past its zenith, and their arrogance is bearing dark fruit. The family provides insight into the decline of the Creole aristocracy, under the pressure of both circumstances and self-destructive pride. An important conflict facing the white Honoré as the story develops is that of the long-standing feud of his family with the De Grapions, whose slender lineage is represented in 1803 by Aurora De Grapion Nancanou and her daughter Clotilde. The rivalry between the two families had begun in the early days of colonial Louisiana, but while the Grandissimes had become numerous and powerful, the De Grapion family tree had risen "as slenderly as a stalk of wild oats."[7] Now the family is reduced to the two women. The self-destructive tendency of the Creole civilization is particularly evident in the destiny of the De Grapions, for the lives of their young men had ended in duels before families could be developed. Aurora's husband was killed in a duel with old Agricola Fusilier, Honoré's uncle. The young Nancanou had lost his plantation to Agricola at cards, after which he had accused him of cheating. The loss of the plantation has left Aurora and Clotilde in poverty which a stiff pride will not let them admit. However, their graciousness, humor and resilience keep them alive (Howells, for one, was charmed by their Creole *joie de vivre*). Honoré is placed in considerable tension by his love for Aurora, since his love is at odds with the families' traditional feud. His move at the end of the novel to restore her plantation, which Agricola had kept out of "honor," is complicated by the impending doom of the Grandissime holdings, for her plantation is one of the few valid titles in the new American regime. Significantly, he returns her plantation, not in the name of love, but for "justice and the fear of God" (p. 262). Honoré comes to realize the wrong done to the De Grapions by the feud and by Grandissime pride.

The conflict between the Grandissimes and the De Grapions is subdued by more fundamental, nastier problems which spring on Honoré and his family out of a heritage of depravity. Honoré is caught in "the length, the blackness" of "the shadow of the Ethiopian." We sit, he says, in a "horrible darkness" (p. 156). Speaking to the immigrant Joseph Frowenfeld, Honoré concludes:

> It is the *Némésis* w'ich, instead of coming afteh, glides along by the side of this morhal, political, commercial, social mistake! It blanches, my-de'-seh, ow whole civilization! It drhags us a centurhy behind the rhes' of the world! It rhetahds and poisons everhy industrhy we got!—mos' of all our-h immense agrhicultu'e! It brheeds a thousan' cusses that nevva leave home but jus' flutter-h up an' rhoost, my-de'-seh, on ow *heads;* an' we nevva know it!—yes, sometimes some of us know it. (p. 156)

Honoré has a literal shadow in the novel, a dark half-brother, also named Honoré Grandissime. The dark Honoré is a free man of color and rich, with extensive holdings inherited from his Grandissime father. Though educated in Paris, the f.m.c. is placed in a cruel social position by his Negro blood, and he is finally driven to suicide. The white Honoré has considerable guilt feelings about the way his dark brother is treated, but he, too, is trapped by family tradition and social pressure. At the end of the novel, he can salvage the Grandissime holdings only by securing the partnership of the f.m.c. While he acknowledges the f.m.c.'s existence by forming the firm of *Grandissime Brothers,* the union ends quickly through the suicide.

In addition to his shadow, the f.m.c., the white Honoré experiences anguish over the cruel treatment of blacks by his family. The best evidence of his agony is the story of Bras-Coupé which he tells to Frowenfeld. Generally regarded as the center of the novel, the Bras-Coupé story's importance is stressed by the fact that it is told three times in the same day. Honoré's telling it to Frowenfeld tells something of his personal burden of the past sins of his family and society. When the giant Bras-Coupé, a Jaloff prince, refuses to work as a slave to the Grandissime family, scenes of violence, pursuit, and torture follow. Bras-Coupé is captured and punished according to the provisions of the Black Code—his hamstrings are cut, his ears cut off, and he is branded with the *fleur de lis.* His defiance takes supernatural dimensions when his curse upon his owner's plantation brings famine, sickness, and death. Though Bras-Coupé lifted his curse before he died, Honoré and his family continue to feel its power. Bras-Coupé means "arm cut off," and the persistent brutality of the Grandissime family toward the f.m.c., the beautiful quadroon Palmyre, and the old slave woman Clemence demonstrates that the family continues not only to destroy the blacks who live among them, but themselves as well. In what is regarded as one of the most successful scenes of the novel, Clemence is caught in a bear trap by family members and is shot and killed when she is later set free. Honoré is not present to stop this violence, but he has perceived how much in error his family traditions are. Early in the novel, he points out Bras-Coupé's grave to Frowenfeld and admits that the "negro's death changed the whole channel of my convictions" (p. 38).

Honoré's determination to liberalize the ways of his family is qualified, however, by his allegiance to their traditional values and his obligation to their ties of blood. The traditions of the Grandissime family are most fully embodied in Agricola Fusilier, Honoré's uncle. Agricola, "the aged high-priest of a doomed civilization,"[8] says he knows the past through tradition, which he believes is more authentic than history. That is, he chooses to believe his family's version of an "ideal past," rather than the real past, and he serves as a symbol of the vain attempt to preserve the past unchanged. Significantly, at the time of the novel Agricola is past his prime, like the Creoles he represents. This transient quality in his character makes him especially appealing. In spite of his hate for Negroes, Americans, or anyone else who opposes his values, his desperate clinging to his family has the effect of giving his character meaning. Cable treats him with considerable sympathy. The positive values Agricola represents—family, a sense of place, friendship, warmth, and personal dignity—are why the white Honoré is peculiarly burdened by the past, for he cannot reject it easily. Significantly, in his deathbed scene, Agricola reaches out specifically to Honoré, as he realizes his values are dying with him: "Oh, Honoré, you and the Yankees—you and—all—going wrong—education—masses—weaken—caste—indiscr—quarrels settl'—by affidav'—Oh! Honoré" (p. 326).

Honoré is thus caught in peculiar contradictory pressures. He sees that "the shadow of the Ethiopian" has far-reaching effects, not only on society, but on his family as well. His realization has a significant personal dimension. His dark brother and Agricola are at odds throughout the novel, and their relationship ends in murder when the f.m.c. knifes Agricola. They are in Frowenfeld's pharmacy, "when Agricola suddenly advanced a step and struck the f.m.c. on the head with his staff. . . . the two crashed together and fell, Agricola above, the f.m.c. below, and a long knife lifted up from underneath and sinking to the hilt, once—twice—thrice,—in the old man's back" (p. 319). This scene is a crude kind of allegory on the state of the Southern social order, and a reiteration of the "arm cut off" motif in the Bras-Coupé story. The two crash to the ground, white man above, black below, but the final impact of the curse is evident: the knife reaches up from underneath and plunges into the old man's back. The shadow destroys the traditional community, its best values as well as its worst.

How the white Honoré puzzles throughout the novel over reconciling the tensions in his family and community is a subject for another essay. The point here, in this introductory paraphrase for readers who may be unacquainted with *The Grandissimes,* is to suggest that his dilemma between "the pull of the old community" and "forces separating him from it" is important to the meaning and strength of the novel.[9] His struggle brings together the two powerful elements in Cable's subject: first, the passing of the old Creole aristocracy after 1803, with its themes of transience and decline under the pressure of circumstances and self-destructive pride; second, the strong political statement about the black-white conflict in the Southern community, a statement that applies to the racial problems of New Orleans and the South after 1865, though its roots are deep in the arrogance of the Southern past. Indeed, Cable makes it plain that *The Grandissimes* was "as political a work as it ever has been called,"[10] and that it "contained as plain a protest against the times in which it was written as against the earlier times in which its scenes were set."[11]

In this context of application to the contemporary South, it is important to recognize, briefly, the relationship of Honoré's dilemma to Cable's own conflict as an artist living and working in the South during Reconstruction. Understanding Cable's own ambivalent attitude toward New Orleans and the South after 1865 provides insight into Honoré's struggle and the resultant power and complexity of the novel. More important, such an understanding might explain, at least in part, something of a recognized flaw in the novel and how it foreshadows Cable's artistic decline after 1880. Cable was already thirty-six years old in 1880, but he continued to write fiction throughout his long life. In all, he would publish fourteen more novels and collections of short fiction, and his last novel *Lovers of Louisiana* was published in 1918, just seven years before his death. Yet *The Grandissimes,* his first novel, was, curiously, his best. A central issue, then, in dealing with Cable as an artist, is to understand his failure, or at best mediocrity, over the long term as well as his success as a beginner. Why was the early promise of *The Grandissimes* not fulfilled?

This is, of course, a complex issue, as Rubin and others have pointed out. Yet not enough has been said, it seems to me, about the tremendous mental and spiritual polarization in the world that Cable knew after 1865. He was caught in a historical moment, Reconstruction, in which the tensions between past and present were expressed dogmatically by what C. Van Woodward calls the "doomed generation," those who remained loyal to the principles of the Old South, and a progressive group who advocated the philosophy of the New South.

Cable's personal crisis is described in his own words: "As I watched the Great Reconstruction agony from its first day to its last, I found my emotions deeply torn—with my sympathies ranged upon the pro-Southern side of the issue and my convictions drifting irresistibly toward the other."[12] Cable did not simply hate the South, or the Creoles, as so many of his contemporaries thought, and some later critics have charged. Nor did his major difficulty spring from his exile to Northampton, though he was removed from the source of his materials. Indeed, he paid an artistic price for continuing to live in New Orleans from 1865 to 1884, where the pull of the old community and the forces separating him from it became polarized. What eventually happened to him may be understood in this analysis by Allen Tate of Ellen Glasgow and James Branch Cabell. Writing to Donald Davidson, Tate says:

> Isn't the point about Cabell and Glasgow this: that because they have a mixed thesis—i.e., mixed of Old Southism and progress—because their intelligences are split into contradictory values, they are bad novelists. This would be literary criticism using the social material to explain the literary deficiency. That is to say, we must attack them first as artists, and then show that their social attitude, because it is muddled, distracts the creative mind into mere propaganda and ruins the work of art. This could almost be made into a principle—that all great or really good writing must have a simple homogeneous sense of values, which incidentally are the kind of values we wish to restore.[13]

In his career after *The Grandissimes*, Cable would finally be unable to reconcile his love for some of the South's values with his abhorrence for some of its evils. Actually, he would perhaps have done well to confine his attention to the chronicle of destruction in Southern history, one aspect of what we see in *The Grandissimes*. Such a chronicle tells us that whatever glorious Southern past there was is irretrievable, and the burden of destruction presses so severely on the present that it is irredeemable. Yet Cable was pressed by strong forces—the doomed generation and the New Southists—to refuse to admit that the past is irretrievable and the present, irredeemable. In his polemical essays, such as *The Silent South*, Cable the reformer and New Southist would assume that the present can be redeemed. In the pastoral *Bonaventure* (1888) and the romances beginning with *The Cavalier* (1901), he would attempt escape through the retrieval of an idyllic past, where the problems of racism are not present. Both his compulsion for social reform and his desire for romantic escape would damage his artistic success.

The Grandissimes springs from a special moment of equilibrium in Cable's career, a moment of balance between sympathy for and judgment on New Orleans and the South. It is Cable's best novel primarily because of this balance. In this moment, which proved to be quite temporary, he was able to examine the connections between the decline of the best values in the Creole community, its self-destructive arrogance, and the far-reaching effects of its sins on the contemporary South. These themes achieve full significance in his creation of Honoré Grandissime, a character with a dilemma much like that of the artist himself. Honoré attempts to reconcile his sympathy for the traditional values of the Southern community, represented here by his own Grandissime family, with his judgments on its evils, especially slavery and racism. Cable's own dilemma of sympathy and judgment would lead inevitably to a schism in his mind and art, primarily because the world of Reconstruction and the New South presented such extreme contradictions in values. The ex-Confederate soldier who had grown up in "New Orleans La Belle," who had returned to it after the war, who had wanted to preserve it so it would not "go so to waste," was caught in a violent milieu of race riots and intense psychological pressure. As his essay "My Politics" reveals, he came to see the shadow in the Southern garden, a perception that gives *The Grandissimes* much of its power. Under the angry, irreconcilable pressure of Reconstruction and the New South, however, he could not maintain his moment of strength, and he turned to the alternatives of sociology, on the one hand, and romantic escape, on the other.

Even in *The Grandissimes*, the reader does not have a perfect novel. There is an uneasy juxtaposition of romance and realism, a mélange of local color, sentiment, and violence, indicating some division in the artist's sensibility. More important, I think, the novel is slightly flawed because Honoré's dilemma is not given the attention it deserves. Honoré shares the stage with Cable's moral voice, Joseph Frowenfeld. In his excellent article, "The 'Double Center': Character and Meaning in Cable's Early Novels," Donald A. Ringe reviews the difficulties in defining Frowenfeld as the single moral spokesman for Cable, pointing out that Honoré speaks for him as well. He believes that Frowenfeld and Honoré learn from each other and that they arrive at the same moral conclusions as the novel develops. In addition, he points out that Frowenfeld is not offered as an entirely serious, moral judge; instead, his highmindedness is treated with some humor, and his naivete is presented with a touch of irony.[14] All this is true, I think. Frowenfeld arrives in New Orleans at the beginning of the novel and is initiated physically by losing all of his family to yellow fever and almost dying of it himself. He slowly learns, and the reader learns with him, about the intricacies of the Grandissime family. We do laugh at his innocence.

Yet, somehow, the fact that Frowenfeld exists at all, or, at least, is given substantial attention is troublesome. He has been compared to Kristian Koppig in the earlier story "Tite Poulette" as a spokesman for that part of Cable who was the Protestant American outsider in New Orleans. Like Koppig, Frowenfeld gives us Cable's social opinions, and he exists primarily to speak out with integrity on the moral issues of the novel. Most important, nothing is made of his internal conflicts, or his taking questions to heart, because his struggle is fundamentally an external one. He is a prophetic voice of judgment on the society he encounters. In that regard, he serves as a conscience to Honoré in his dilemma, offering advice in several interviews as the story develops. Indeed, when Honoré is at the height of his conflict over reparation, one of the visions he has is of Frowenfeld's face. Cable himself lamented over Frowenfeld, writing to Howells that he had failed to portray his goodness artistically and that he was too good to be real. In addition, Rubin points out that Frowenfeld's character is not clearly conceived: he says very critical things about the Creole world, but marries into its society (Clotilde) without any qualms; also, he, a poor immigrant, marries a rich Creole heiress.[15]

In any case, by giving Frowenfeld the space that he does, Cable overlooked the substantial artistic possibilities in developing Honoré's character more fully. He would also fail to see the full significance of the internal dilemmas between sympathy for the old community and judgment on it in Père Jerome's character in *Madame Delphine* and John Richling's in *Dr. Sevier*. Frowenfeld's character does flaw *The Grandissimes*, I think, in spite of his importance in its action, because he exists outside the novel's major themes. He finally offers us what Allen Tate calls "mere propaganda" and a too-easy solution to Honoré's problem. In my judgment, Cable was pressed for a solution to that problem by the tremendous pressures of Reconstruction and the New South. As a result, Frowenfeld pushes the novel in two directions: toward sociology, for he functions as a moral absolute who would "redeem" the South, representing progress as opposed to traditional values; and toward sentiment, as a melodramatic "good" in the fight against "evil." For all the irony with which he is treated, he is essentially a serious, and flat character. He has little difficulty in dealing with the thorny problems at the novel's center because his judgment is the answer. Fortunately, the reader also has the powerful themes embodied in Honoré's realization of how the past affects the present, and they are enough to make *The Grandissimes* one of the classics of Southern fiction.

The six essays included in this special feature add significantly to the body of criticism available on *The Grandissimes*. The variety of topics they examine underscores the richness of the novel. In the opening essay, Donald A. Ringe demonstrates that the narrative voice of the novel is a means of making its strong material acceptable to readers. "An individual voice" who "assumes a personality of his own," the narrator draws the reader into the story and establishes the prevailing comic tone of the early chapters; at the same time, the voice "lays the groundwork for the powerful themes that emerge only toward the close of the novel," and their contemporary application. Next, Alfred Bendixen examines the "modern" qualities of *The Grandissimes*, especially in relation to the earlier plantation tradition in Southern literature. He finds that the novel offers a "new path" for Southern fiction, one which confronts a series of difficult conflicts and particular questions, and one which leads to a better understanding of Southern history.

In "*The Grandissimes* and the French Quarter," Kenneth Holditch and Drayton Hamilton provide readers with a delightful and unique experience: a photographic essay on Cable's house on Eighth Street and on a variety of locations in the Quarter which are important in the novel. The text accompanying the photographs offers historical information on the locations as well as comment on Cable's use of them. Next, William Bedford Clark looks at the important topic of humor in *The Grandissimes* and finds that it plays a remarkably complex role. Firmly rooted in the traditions of local color and the comedy of manners, Cable's comic vision defines the structure and balance of the novel, offering relief and sweetening the moral. More important, however, humor in *The Grandissimes* has much darker implications. Cable's laughter, often biting and ironic, gives artistic distance from the brutal subject matter and provides artistic control over anger and condemnation. Lawrence Berkove's scholarly essay focuses on the free man of color motif in *The Grandissimes* and works by Joel Chandler Harris and Mark Twain, especially "Free Joe" and Huckleberry Finn. Not claiming direct influence, Berkove points out that the "signal prominence" Cable gave "to the shadowy figure of Honoré Grandissime, f.m.c." brought on a "literary awakening" in the 1880s to the plight of people of color recently freed in Reconstruction. Cable's use of the f.m.c. is thus not sentimental but political as he initiated protest against the "post-Reconstruction move in the South to abridge the rights of black freedmen." In the concluding essay, Joseph Egan compares Agricola Fusilier and Bras-Coupé in *The Grandissimes* and finds that they are in the tradition of antithetical doubles—opposing characters who are used to reveal symbolic truth. Cable characterizes both as aristocratic "lions" in their violent opposition to each other and in their similar deaths. Most important, as Egan shows, "these warring lions, each the victim of virulent prejudice, give emphatic testimony to the manifold destruction—and self-destruction—accompanying malice and intolerance."

Citations from the text of *The Grandissimes* in each essay are from the Hill and Wang edition (1957), since it remains in print and is readily available to readers.

Finally, I wish to thank Peggy W. Prenshaw, editor of the *Southern Quarterly,* for her commitment to this special feature on *The Grandissimes.* Her initial encouragement, editorial supervision, and critical judgment deserve appreciation. In addition, I owe special thanks to

Cheryl Saunders, whose knowledge of printing, hard work on the manuscripts, and generous contributions of time made the idea of a collection of centennial essays become a reality.

University of Southern Mississippi   Thomas J. Richardson

NOTES

[1]Merrill M. Skaggs, *The Folk of Southern Fiction* (Athens: Univ. of Georgia Press, 1972), p. 154.

[2]See especially Richard Chase, "Cable's *Grandissimes*," in *The American Novel and Its Tradition* (Garden City, N.Y.: Doubleday, 1957), pp. 167–76; Newton Arvin, Introduction to *The Grandissimes* (New York: Sagamore Press, 1957; Hill and Wang, 1957), pp. v–xi; Jay Martin, "Paradises Lost," in *Harvests of Change: American Literature, 1865–1914* (Englewood Cliffs, N.J.: Prentice-Hall, 1967); pp. 81–105; Louis D. Rubin, Jr., *George W. Cable: The Life and Times of a Southern Heretic* (New York: Pegasus, 1969), pp. 77–96. In addition, the reader should see Philip Butcher, *George Washington Cable* (New York: Twayne, 1962); Edmund Wilson, "The Ordeal of George Washington Cable," in *Patriotic Gore: Studies in the American Civil War* (New York: Oxford Univ. Press, 1962); Elmo Howell, "George Washington Cable's Creoles: Art and Reform in *The Grandissimes*," *Mississippi Quarterly*, 26 (1973), 43–53; John Cleman, "The Art of Local Color in George W. Cable's *The Grandissimes*," *American Literature*, 47 (1975), 396–410; William Bedford Clark, "Cable and the Theme of Miscegenation in *Old Creole Days* and *The Grandissimes*," *Mississippi Quarterly*, 30 (1977), 597–609; Richard Bozman Eaton, "George W. Cable and the Historical Romance," *The Southern Literary Journal*, 8 (1975), 82–94; and Robert O. Stephens, "Cable's *The Grandissimes* and the Comedy of Manners," *American Literature*, 51 (1980) 507–19.

[3]Chase, pp. 167–68.

[4]Rubin, p. 78.

[5]Rubin, p. 79.

[6]Cited in Arlin Turner, *George W. Cable: A Biography* (Durham: Duke Univ. Press, 1956), p. 90.

[7]*The Grandissimes* (New York: Hill and Wang, 1957), p. 23. Hereafter, all citations in the text are to page numbers in this edition.

[8]For a fuller discussion of Agricola, see Martin, p. 104.

[9]See Louis D. Rubin, Jr., *The Writer in the South* (Athens: Univ. of Georgia Press, 1970), for an analysis of this tension in the life and art of Mark Twain.

[10]"My Politics," in *The Negro Question*, ed. Arlin Turner (New York: W. W. Norton, 1958), p. 14.

[11]Cable's diary, cited in Newton Arvin, Introduction, *The Grandissimes* (New York: Hill and Wang, 1957), p. viii.

[12]Cited in C. Van Woodward, *Origins of the New South, 1877–1913* (Baton Rouge: Louisiana State Univ. Press, 1951), p. 164.

[13]Allen Tate, "The Agrarian Symposium, Letters of Allen Tate and Donald Davidson, 1928–30," ed. by John Tyree Fain and Thomas Daniel Young, *Southern Review*, 8 (1972), 875.

[14]"The 'Double Center': Character and Meaning in Cable's Early Novels," *Studies in the Novel*, 5 (1973), 52–62.

[15]*George W. Cable: The Life and Times of A Southern Heretic*, pp. 44–45.

Narrative Voice in Cable's *The Grandissimes*

DONALD A. RINGE

As a Southern writer who held unorthodox opinions on the racial question, George Washington Cable faced a difficult problem in writing *The Grandissimes:* how to make an unpopular theme palatable to an audience, Northern as well as Southern, that did not share his views. The local color so lavishly spread throughout the book would, Cable knew, undoubtedly help win readers, for the tales of Creole New Orleans that he had published in *Scribner's Monthly* since 1873 and had collected in *Old Creole Days* (1879) had been successful. But his most serious treatment of racial injustice, "The Story of Bras-Coupé," had not been accepted by the editors of Northern magazines when Cable had tried to publish it as a short story. In several forms it had been rejected by a number of editors, including Richard Watson Gilder of *Scribner's Monthly* and George Parsons Lathrop of the *Atlantic,* who objected to "the unmitigatedly distressful effect of the story."[1] Since "The Story of Bras-Coupé" was to be at both the physical and intellectual center of *The Grandissimes,*[2] Cable had to find a way to make the material acceptable to his readers.[3]

He found the means in the narrative voice through which the novel is told. One notices at once, in the very first paragraphs of the book, the conversational tone that the narrator uses as he begins to describe the masquerade ball with which the novel opens:

> It was in the Théatre St. Philippe (they had laid a temporary floor over the parquette seats) in the city we now call New Orleans, in the month of September, and in the year 1803. . . . For summer there, bear in mind, is a loitering gossip, that only begins to talk of leaving when September rises to go. It was like hustling her out, it is true, to give a select *bal masqué* at such a very early—such an amusingly early date; but it was fitting that something should be done for the sick and the destitute; and why not this? Everybody knows the Lord loveth a cheerful giver.

13

And so, to repeat, it was in the Théatre St. Philippe (the oldest, the first one), and, as may have been noticed, in the year in which the First Consul of France gave away Louisiana. Some might call it "sold."[4]

This is not an objective third person narration.[5] The passage is "spoken" by an individual voice which, through his many asides, his emphases, his rhetorical question, and his mild irony, assumes a personality of his own.

The device was a happy one. Because he addresses an audience of 1880 that, he assumes, would like to hear about New Orleans life of some seventy-five years before, the narrative voice appeals on one level, to readers of historical romance. He explains in detail the geographical peculiarities of the city, points out the changes that time has wrought in it, and describes with fondness and humor the people who, to Anglo-Saxon readers of 1880, must have seemed alien and strange. The mixture of races—black, Indian, and white—that makes up the social organization, the complex racial attitudes that both bind the various groups together and create a tension among them, the extended family connections among the Creoles, the fierce family pride and equally fierce family feuds that derive from it—all are described in abundant realistic detail. The narrator gives readers a densely drawn picture of Creole society and reproduces precisely the language the characters speak: Creole French, the black patois, and various kinds of Gallic-English, a dialect that must have disconcerted many American readers as they tried to thread their way through the dialogue.

The narrative voice makes heavy demands on readers, but also draws them consciously into the story. At one point, he pauses to observe: "Here is the way they talked in New Orleans in those days. If you care to understand why Louisiana has grown up so out of joint, note the tone of those who governed her in the middle of the last century" (p. 26). At another, he depicts the house of Aurora and Clotilde Nancanou as the modest dwelling it is, but, as if in fear that he might create the wrong impression with the description, he quickly adds: "Yet if you hastily picture to yourself a forlorn-looking establishment, you will be moving straight away from the fact" (p. 62). At yet another, he describes the house of the Grandissimes during the *fête de grandpère* and says in a brief aside: "Do not look for it now; it is quite gone" (p. 158). By these means, the narrator establishes himself as a person thoroughly knowledgeable about the material he is presenting, but also as one who is able to maintain a close rapport with his audience.

He even affects concern for readers by breaking into his story to clarify incidents and explain important details. He points up the significance of a brief scene with the explicit statement: "We may add here an incident which seemed, when it took place, as unimportant as a single fact well could be" (p. 42); and he breaks into his narrative, even in mid-sentence, to present some necessary background information: "He handed the apothecary—but a few words in time, lest we misjudge." He then describes, in a long, two-page paragraph, some essential facts about the Grandissime family, and picks up the narrative again in almost the same words as the suspended statement: "The landlord handed the apothecary the following writing" (pp. 108–09). The narrator even includes a description which assumes in one of its details that readers are visibly before him! "She had lost— alas! how can we communicate it in English!—a small piece of lute- string ribbon, about *so long,* which she used for—not a necktie exactly, but—" (p. 131). The narrative voice is a conscious story teller who orders the events of the book and controls the manner in which they are told.

The retrospective narration, for example, is told primarily by the narrator, who presents it in his own voice, but he maintains the fiction that one character—Charlie Keene, or Honoré Grandissime, among others—is actually, in the universe of the novel, explaining things to Joseph Frowenfeld, a newcomer to New Orleans. The narrative voice usually begins with that dialogue, then intervenes to summarize what is being told. In two instances, however, he interrupts the narration with a brief bit of dialogue between the two characters to remind readers that what they are reading as straight narrative is simultane- ously being told by one character to another (pp. 28, 191). In effect, the narrative voice merges with the character who is explaining Creole society and the history of the Creole families to Joseph Frowenfeld; and readers assume the position of Frowenfeld as uninstructed stran- gers who must be informed about such matters if they are to under- stand what is going on around them.[6] Readers are made to sympathize with Frowenfeld, to see things, to some extent at least, from his point of view, and to come to awareness with him of the reality he is witnessing. The identification is not complete, but it is sometimes close.

Other techniques are equally subtle. Though most of the story is told through the use of past tense verbs ("Joseph was . . .," "Frowenfeld did . . .," "Honoré said . . ."), the narrator sometimes slips without warning into brief passages of present-tense description. At the *bal masqué* that opens the novel, a single paragraph is presented in this manner: "An hour has passed by. The dance goes on; hearts are beating, wit is flashing. . . . But the Monk and the Huguenotte are not on the floor. They are sitting where they have been left by their two companions, in one of the boxes of the theater, looking out upon the unwearied whirl and flash of gauze and light and color" (p. 3). The technique appears again in a number of descriptions: of the Nancanou household (pp. 62–63, 68–69), of Frowenfeld and his surroundings as he sits in meditation on the levee (pp. 78–79), of the *fête de grandpère* at the Grandissime mansion (pp. 162–64), of Bras-Coupé in the swamp (p. 182), and of the scene on the Place d'Armes, in the next to last chapter, where the major characters are brought together for the final time (pp. 332–33). In all of these descriptions, the narrator brings the action into the timeless present and gives each episode a sense of immediacy that it would not otherwise have had.

The narrative voice is most effective, however, in establishing the tone of the book. Cable was apparently very much aware that he had to control readers' initial response to the material if he was to retain interest throughout the book and win, if not complete acceptance, at least understanding of the themes he wished to develop. In this matter, the narrative voice served him well. The novel opens in a light comic vein. Though serious problems are hinted at, the comedy is maintained throughout the first half of the book. Most of the Creole men are drawn with comic exaggeration to point up their moral attitudes and personal and family pride. The narrator even assumes their point of view at times to reveal their attitudes with the properly comic note. Thus, of their racial attitudes, he writes: "the true, main Grandissime stock . . . has kept itself lily-white ever since France has

loved lilies—as to marriage, that is; as to less responsible entanglements, why, of course—" (p. 22). In a similar fashion, he reveals
their family pride in comic asides, as, for example: "M. De Grapion
would not sell her. (Trade with a Grandissime? Let them suspect he
needed money?) No" (p. 60).

He even pokes fun at so attractive a character as Aurora Nancanou.
She shares the superstition of most of the Creoles and engages in
voudou practice with Palmyre Philosophe, the quadroon woman with
whom she was reared, to make a love charm. Her experience is
presented in an essentially comic manner, as is her resolve to give up
such practices, "except, to be sure, . . . such ordinary precautions
against misfortune as casting upon the floor a little of whatever she
might be eating or drinking to propitiate M. Assonquer" (pp. 130–31).
The narrator also enters her mind to reveal her family pride and
personal vanity: "Do you suppose she was going to put on the face of
having been born or married to this degraded condition of things?" (p.
64); or, "Clotilde was a dear daughter—ha! few women were capable
of having such a daughter as Clotilde" (p. 129). Though the narrator is
unsparing of Creole faults and follies, he presents them usually with a
comic or lightly ironic touch that amuses readers who hear their comic
dialogue, observe their dramatic posturing, and try to understand
their moral and social attitudes.

But the comic tone is not reserved for the Creoles alone. Even
Joseph Frowenfeld, who, we know, reflects the author's social and
moral opinions, is treated with humor. The studious apothecary—an
"escaped book-worm," as the narrator calls him (p. 91)—is slow to
perceive what is going on around him, but he is passionate in defense
of abstract principle. Personal relations escape him: he fails to find out
for himself that there are two Honoré Grandissimes, and that the
Nancanou women are mother and daughter, not sisters, as he had
supposed. Others must reveal both facts to him. He cuts a ludicrous
figure in his angry response to the injustice he perceives in New
Orleans society, and he is especially comic when he expounds his
ideas to Aurora and Clotilde, who do not fully understand what he is
saying, but who, out of politeness, pretend to agree with him, even
when their assent goes directly against their convictions. The high,

impersonal—even inhuman—moral stand he invariably takes is as much the object of the narrator's irony as are the vanity, pride, and moral obtuseness of the Creoles.[7]

Serious matters are introduced, of course, in the first half of the book: the stabbing of Agricola Fusilier, for example, the wounding of Palmyre, his assailant, and the hopeless love that the second Honoré Grandissime, the free man of color, bears for her. But these events are kept very much in the background, the attempted murder leads to no fatal results, and even these serious personal relations have their comic aspects: as when Palmyre attempts to put a voudou curse on Agricola by sitting in the place he has just occupied, or when the free man of color, mistaking the apothecary for a sorcerer, asks him for a *ouangan* so that he may win the love of Palmyre. Frowenfeld, on his part, can hardly believe that intelligent Creoles actually practice voudou, and he is horrified at the use to which some basil he has sold Aurora is to be put. Readers, of course, are not likely to take such matters seriously, and probably smile as well at the general Creole attitude toward the apothecary, whom most of them dislike and some half-fear as an astrologer or magician.

As soon as he introduces the story of Bras-Coupé, however, the narrator changes his tone. In an extended metaphor, dripping with savage irony, he describes the African slaves as commodities, as merchandise that sometimes "failed to keep" when it was shipped across the ocean (p. 169). He reveals the just cause of Palmyre's hatred of Agricola Fusilier in the cruelty of the fierce old Creole, who forced her marriage to Bras-Coupé, and he lays before readers all the horrors of slavery, the inhumanity of the *Code Noir,* and the terrible punishment Bras-Coupé suffers for simply seeking his rights as a man. By presenting the story of Bras-Coupé at just this point, the precise center of the book, the narrator throws all that has gone before into a new relation and gives the book a much darker tone. Once the story is told, moreover, the narrative voice slips into the background, and the latter half of the novel is told in something more closely approaching the objective third person type of narration. The narrative voice, as we shall see, does not disappear completely, but seems intent, rather, on letting the theme be perceived in the events themselves—events that contrast sharply with those in the first half of the book.

The traits of Creole character once perceived as comic now reveal their ugly aspects. Personal pride leads to a threatened duel between Agricola Fusilier and his nephew, Sylvestre Grandissime, a duel that is avoided only with considerable difficulty. And family pride and racial arrogance result in violence and death when Honoré Grandissime decides to right a pair of wrongs that have been committed by his family. He holds title to a plantation once gambled away to Agricola Fusilier by Aurora's dead husband, who was killed in a duel after falsely accusing Agricola of cheating. Agricola was willing to return the plantation to the widow if she would admit that it had been won honestly, but she, in her pride, refused to do so. Honoré breaks the impasse by making the deed over to her, but, to protect the Grandissime interests, which cannot prosper without the wealth of that plantation, he accepts a sum of money from his quadroon half-brother—the second Honoré Grandissime—and accedes to the condition that his business be renamed "Grandissime Brothers." This double violation of Creole prejudice causes an immediate uproar.

A lynch mob seeks out the black Honoré and, finding him not at home, ransacks his house. Passing the apothecary shop, moreover, which Frowenfeld rents from the free man of color, the mob takes out its hostility toward both men by smashing the windows and destroying Frowenfeld's stock in trade. Worse, some months later, when Agricola happens to meet the black Honoré in Frowenfeld's shop, he takes his cane to him and is mortally stabbed in return. Meanwhile, Palmyre Philosophe has sought revenge on Agricola for the wrongs he has done her. She sends Clemence, the *marchande des calas*, at night to place voudou charms of death about him. Clemence is caught in a steel trap by Jean-Baptiste Grandissime, who has lain in wait for her, and as the Creole men gather, she pleads for her life, denying all knowledge of the black arm made of wax—a *bras-coupé*—that she was carrying in a small coffin. In a scene of unusual cruelty, the Creoles first string her up, then let her down and tell her to run for her life. But as she stumbles off, they shoot her in her tracks. Even the voudou charms, at first presented comically in terms of love, turn sinister as the story darkens.

The attractive characters, too, are shown in a more somber light. In one brief incident, just before Honoré arrives to relieve their distress,

Aurora and Clotilde both shed their frivolous ways and comic dialect—they are speaking French, which the narrator renders as standard English—to discuss the awkward position in which society has placed them. As ladies, they may not work. Hence, as Clotilde puts it, their problem "is not how to make a living, but how to get a living without making it" (p. 255). At first it is the more serious Clotilde who protests their fate, but even the ebullient Aurora for once lays aside her social mask to speak in a serious voice: "I will tell you the honest truth; some days when I get very, very hungry, and we have nothing but rice—all because we are ladies without male protectors—I think society could drive even me to marriage!" (p. 255). Though Aurora quickly resumes her usual manner and the book ends happily with a double betrothal—Honoré to Aurora, and Frowenfeld to Clotilde—for one short moment, we are allowed to see the harsh reality that an aristocratic society has imposed upon these women.

Joseph Frowenfeld also learns the power of social opinion. The high moral stand he always assumes in his criticism of Creole society makes him especially vulnerable to attack at the first sign of frailty on his part, and once he appears to have fallen, the Creoles show him no mercy. Visiting the home of Palmyre on legitimate business, he is aghast to see her fall on her knees and beg for a charm to win the love of the white Honoré. Her African woman misunderstands what is happening, and, thinking that she is protecting Palmyre, strikes the apothecary with a piece of wood. He staggers into the street with a bloody head just as several Creole men are passing. They, of course, put the worst possible interpretation on the incident: they blacken his name with gossip about his attempt to seduce the beautiful quadroon. Frowenfeld feels intensely the loss of his reputation, but he is powerless to defend himself until Palmyre clears his name. Though the incident certainly has its comic aspect, its effects are extremely serious. It brings into the open the Creoles' deep animosity toward the liberal *Américain,* and it helps them justify the sacking of his shop.

While all these events are transpiring, the narrative voice rarely breaks into the action. When he does, he too is much more serious than he has heretofore been. In "The Story of Bras-Coupé," he begins to draw parallels between the world of 1800 and that of 1880, suggesting at one point: "We have a *Code Noir* now, but the new one is a mental reservation, not an enactment" (p. 181). He points out that, then as now, Southerners like to believe their slaves were "the happiest people under the sun" (p. 249), and he observes, more broadly, how unpleasant it is "to see the comfortable fractions of Christian communities everywhere striving, with sincere, pious, well-meant, criminal benevolence, to make their poor brethren contented with the ditch" (p. 251). As the story itself darkens, the narrative voice makes clear that his theme applies as much to Anglo-Saxon attitudes in his own day as it does to Creole New Orleans at the time of the American accession (pp. 329–30). Assuming the tone and opinions of Cable himself, he reminds readers of 1880 that the problems he has presented in terms of the past are very much a part of their own world.[8]

By the end of the novel, Cable has brought readers a long way from the local color, historical romance with light social commentary that the opening chapters seem to promise them. Through the use of the narrative voice in the first half of the book, he locates readers in time and place, leads them through the labyrinth of Creole society, amuses them with the comic depiction of the characters, and lays the groundwork for the powerful themes that emerge only toward the close of the novel. Once he has won readers' attention and interest, he presents them with the shocking tale of Bras-Coupé to epitomize the grave injustice that lay at the heart of Creole society. The effect is dramatic. It forces readers to see the characters in a new and more serious context and wins their assent to the theme of racial injustice which the tale and its tragic consequences so clearly reveal. Lest readers assume, however, that the theme applies only to the world of 1804, the narrative voice intervenes to remind them of its contemporary application. Readers are ready to accept that suggestion: they have been well prepared by the manner in which the novel has been presented.

NOTES

[1]Arlin Turner, *George W. Cable: A Biography* (Durham, N. C.: Duke Univ. Press, 1956), p. 54. At the time of its rejection, the story was entitled "Bibi."

[2]Cf. Louis D. Rubin, Jr., *George W. Cable: The Life and Times of a Southern Heretic* (New York: Pegasus, 1969), p. 81. Cable himself saw *The Grandissimes* "as an expansion of the Bras-Coupé story." See Lucy L. C. Biklé, *George W. Cable: His Life and Letters* (New York: Charles Scribner's Sons, 1928), p. 180.

[3]According to Turner, Cable had included more explicit discussions of slavery in

the early drafts of the novel, but reduced them in successive revisions—evidence that he was indeed concerned with the strategy of presentation of his material. See Turner, p. 93.

[4]*The Grandissimes* (New York: Hill and Wang, 1957), p. 1. Hereafter, all citations are to page numbers in this edition.

[5]Cf. Richard Bozman Eaton, "George W. Cable and the Historical Romance," *The Southern Literary Journal*, 8 (Fall 1975), 89–91. Although Eaton notes that "lightness of touch, whimsy, even some slight frenzy" characterize the narration of Chapter I and that Chapters IV and V are told in a "charmingly tongue-in-cheek" manner, he believes the novel is presented in Cable's "own person." I think, rather, that a distinction must be made between Cable as author and the narrative voice of the book.

[6]Cf. John Cleman, "The Art of Local Color in George W. Cable's *The Grandissimes*," *American Literature*, 47 (1975), 399; Eaton, p. 91.

[7]For a discussion of this aspect of Frowenfeld's character and his relation to Honoré Grandissime, see my article "The 'Double Center': Character and Meaning in Cable's Early Novel," *Studies in the Novel*, 5 (Spring 1973), 54–58.

[8]Cf. Turner, p. 93, and Rubin, p. 84, both of whom draw parallels between the New Orleans of the American accession and that of Reconstruction. In the last passage quoted above, however, Cable implies that his theme goes beyond these local conditions.

Cable's *The Grandissimes:*
A Literary Pioneer Confronts The Southern Tradition

There was a well-established Southern literary tradition when George W. Cable's *The Grandissimes* appeared in 1880, but it was a tradition devoted to stifling any criticism of the South. One could find something resembling an honest account of life in the works of the Southwestern humorists, but these works were generally regarded as subliterary. The plantation myth that formed the core of what was regarded as "serious" Southern writing tended to ignore or gloss over the realities of slavery. The owners of plantations appeared as gracious and benevolent masters devoted to the welfare of their happy darkies. Southern fiction was more likely to show a slave refusing the offer of freedom and asserting his enjoyment of servitude than to present slave families divided on the auction block. In these books, Northern visitors were more likely to be converted to Southern ways of life than to call for change. As Louis D. Rubin, Jr. has shown, the defensiveness that marked nineteenth-century Southern writing induced even writers of talent to sacrifice artistic truth to the purposes of propaganda.[1]

The plantation myth had its origin in such antebellum works as John Pendleton Kennedy's *Swallow Barn* (1832, revised 1851) and Caroline Lee Hentz's *The Planter's Northern Wife* (1854), but Southern propaganda had its greatest success in the period after the Civil War. By 1880, the efforts of the Northern radicals to impose racial equality on the South had clearly failed. Northerners were more concerned with healing the old wounds left by the war than with seeing that the freed slaves received fair treatment. Carpetbaggers and scalawags provoked more disdain than former confederates. Soon,

Thomas Nelson Page's "Marse Chan" would make even former abolitionists weep, and Albion Tourgée, whose novel, *A Fool's Errand* (1876), offered the most effective attack on Southern racism since Stowe's *Uncle Tom's Cabin,* would lament that American writing had become "not only southern in type, but distinctly Confederate in sympathy."[2]

Confronted with rapid change and the haste of industrialized life, late nineteenth-century readers eagerly retreated into the pastoral world offered by Southern writing, a world that ignored the realities of the present, and romanticized the past. These readers were charmed by the discovery that life had once been graceful and leisurely; for them, the phrase, "the burden of the past," would have had little meaning. What history seemed to teach was that the past had been simpler and easier, that men had been nobler and kinder. Literature was an escape from time, and history was reduced to nostalgia.

But George W. Cable was no escapist. His stories in *Old Creole Days* placed a romantic haze over New Orleans, but he knew that beauty, charm, and grace could mask indolence, hypocrisy, and deceit. He faced the realities of racial injustice and refused to blink. As a reformer, Cable was out of step with the South and most of the nation. The result was the eventual loss of his literary reputation. Reviewers in the 1880s favorably compared him to the finest authors in America and Europe, but when he died in 1925, he was virtually forgotten. Although he seems to have had little direct influence on the major writers of the Southern Renaissance, with whom he is now often compared, critics are justified in praising him as the first modern Southern writer. One of Cable's most astute critics, Louis D. Rubin, Jr., has written:

> In an important sense, *The Grandissimes* may be said to be the first "modern" Southern novel. For if the modern Southern novel has been characterized by its uncompromising attempt to deal honestly with the complexity of Southern racial experience, then *The Grandissimes* was the first important work of fiction written by a Southerner in which that intention is manifested. In this respect, Cable opened up the path along which Ellen Glasgow, William Faulkner, Thomas Wolfe, Robert Penn Warren, Eudora Welty, William Styron, and others would follow.[3]

The modern spirit of *The Grandissimes* goes far beyond Cable's willingness to treat the issue of race or to expose the violence and injustice that characterized the worst aspects of Southern life. If Cable seems modern, it is largely because he approached the South with the critical detachment of a Faulkner instead of with the nostalgia of a Page. Like the great Southern writers of the twentieth century, he had a rich sense of history and knew that the present always had to face the problems of the past. Moreover, like them, he was consciously a literary experimenter who recognized that the old forms of fiction were inadequate and that the complexities of Southern life required a new and complex kind of writing.

Unfortunately, Cable's achievement does not match that of the best Southern writers in our century. In spite of its dramatic force and imaginative power, *The Grandissimes* is too often marred by lapses into prose that is sentimental, preachy, and sometimes even clumsy. Nevertheless, Cable was a true literary pioneer who tried to explore and enlarge the possibilities of fiction. Those who have attempted to classify *The Grandissimes* have generally spoken of it as a mixture of poetic melodrama and social realism, but it has been called everything from an historical romance to a comedy of manners.[4] There seems to be some agreement that H.H. Boyesen was right in predicting that the book would "be the kind of novel which the Germans call 'Kulturroman,' a novel in which the struggling forces of opposing civilizations crystalize [sic] & in which they find their enduring monument."[5] Scholars have been less likely to note Boyesen's feeling that Cable had enough material for "a dozen novels, all tolerably unhackneyed."[6] Cable himself recognized the ambitiousness of his project: "I have grasped at so much. It is the wild, virgin soil that I have to break up; a field never plowed before. The Creole character, the Creole society, the philosophy of these things, Creole errors and defects & how to mend them, all clamoring to be treated by a tyro in a love story."[7]

In 1894, Cable described his attempt to introduce "personalities new to the world of fiction" into "the very old and familiar" story of "a feud between two families."[8] Yet he was interested in doing much more than simply telling a story. In a letter to Boyesen, he proclaimed "that the great problem of a novel should be something beyond and above the mere puzzle of the plot, something great and thought-compelling, that teaches without telling, that brings to view without pointing, that guides without leading and allures without fatiguing, through the dimness and shadow and uncertainty of a new path out at last upon the illimitable savannahs of God's sweet, green, nourishing truth."[9]

In spite of the overwrought prose, the metaphor of the new path seems to me the most revealing of Cable's comments on his own art. Like the modern Southern writers, Cable realized that to tell the truth he had to take risks. Although the modern reader may feel that Cable offers too much telling, pointing, and leading, *The Grandissimes* certainly demands more from the reader than most novels of the period. Cable may interject an occasional ironic comment, but he delays presenting critical information and places the reader into "an atmosphere of hints, allusions, faint unspoken admissions, ill-concealed antipathies, unfinished speeches, mistaken identities and whisperings of hidden strife."[10] The metaphor of the journey through "dimness and shadow" is particularly appropriate since it seems to allude to the second chapter of the book which describes the Frowenfeld family's journey to New Orleans. Expecting a paradise, the family finds instead: "A land hung in mourning, darkened by gigantic cypresses, submerged; a land of reptiles, silence, shadow, decay" (p. 9). They discover a world that quickly kills those who fail to become acclimated. The family's journey is also the reader's journey into the novel, into a strange fictional world that had never been adequately described before; it is a journey that confounds and contradicts pleasant expectations, a journey that challenges the reader as much as it does Frowenfeld.

The goal of the journey is a better and truer understanding of the South, which, as Cable knew, meant an understanding of history. Cable was the first Southern writer fully to understand how the past shaped the present; history could help him explain "why Louisiana has grown up so out of joint" (p. 26). More important, however, he knew how to use the past to define the present, to create a work that "contained as plain a protest against the times in which it was written as against the earlier times in which its scenes were set."[11] The action of the novel covers a period of one year, beginning in September, 1803, but the characters tell stories dating back to the first settlers. In September, 1803, New Orleans was still under the nominal control of the Spanish, although an agreement to transfer the colony to France had been concluded, and rumors of Napoleon's intent to sell his newly gained possession to the United States were already circulating. French control lasted only from November 30 to December 20, when the Americans took command. Thus, the citizens of New Orleans were compelled to change their national allegiance rapidly.

This moment in history provided Cable with an ideal means of examining the issues of Reconstruction. In both periods, proud aristocrats, who were used to depending on slave labor, were forced to accept their membership in a nation that claimed to value freedom and democracy. In both cases, the transition involved the imposition of a military governor with broad powers. Land titles were in doubt, and the direction of political and economic change was unclear. Tension was increased by the influx of new settlers who hoped to take advantage of the situation. Although faced with the need to accept change in their forms of government and ways of life, the Creoles, like the ex-Confederates, were more likely to cling to the customs of the past. Those willing to cooperate with the new government were widely regarded as traitors. Eventually, the Creoles grudgingly accepted their place in the union, declaring they would make their wants known to the central government in Washington—just as Reconstruction Southerners did. However, although white Southerners were ultimately reconciled to the new ways of life, in both cases the issue of racial justice remained unresolved, and blacks continued to be the victims of oppression. Cable's fidelity to historical truth thus demanded a complex plot involving many conflicts, some of which had to remain unresolved. Rejecting the plantation myth's simplistic glorification of the simple and uncomplicated past, *The Grandissimes* insists that all moments of history, both past and present, are difficult and demanding.

As his history, *The Creoles of Louisiana,* demonstrates, Cable believed firmly in progress. Denying the myth of decline in that work, he urged the Creoles to gain a "pride of ascent," a pride in the ways in which nineteenth-century man is better than his ancestors.[12] Like Frowenfeld, Cable wanted the South "to follow the course of modern thought" (p. 143). While the plantation myth affirmed nostalgia and the values of a simple, leisurely life, Cable believed in the gospel of work. Although he was too critical an observer of the New South to accept Henry W. Grady's views, Cable was more likely to praise a hardworking storekeeper than an idle planter. In *The Grandissimes*, the Creoles who best survive the effects of change do so because they can adapt to new economic conditions and overcome their disdain for commerce and "hard and patient labor" (p. 141). It is not surprising that in his later life, Cable became a good friend of Andrew Carnegie.

In Cable's novel, as in many of Faulkner's works, a character's foolish admiration for the past is subject to the author's more critical examination, an examination that often undercuts the character's pride in his ancestry. Agricola Fusilier may take delight in his descent from Lufki-Humma, the Indian princess, but Cable shows us a young girl, unloved by her savage father, who becomes the pawn of the manipulating Listening Crane until she runs off with the first white men she sees and becomes the prize in a game of dice. The first settlers may have had a vast amount of courage, but as Cable shows in this novel and in *The Creoles of Louisiana*, they often lacked humanity. One of the lessons of the past is the need to adapt to change. Fusilier, who glorifies the past instead of learning from it, is ironically much like Listening Crane, an old and foolish man who cannot accept the destruction of his ambitions and dreams.

History in *The Grandissimes* is not to be worshiped but confronted and rectified; the past presents more burdens than blessings. Honoré Grandissime must assume responsibility for his father's actions and for his family's past mistakes. He courageously restores the plantation to Aurora and Clotilde and attempts to give his partially black half-brother the recognition his family would deny. Yet, as the Bras-Coupé story shows, the past is not so easily overcome. The powerful story ends with the mutilated slave feeling the touch of a baby and removing his curse from the land. The story, the most commented on and praised section of the novel, seems to be one in which forgiveness replaces vengeance. Although such a theme indicates Cable's ultimate hope, the book clearly shows that the curse has not been fully lifted. Palmyre still thirsts for revenge, and the compulsion to tell and retell the story shows that Bras-Coupé still haunts the imagination of both blacks and whites in the novel, just as the sins of the past continue to haunt the present.

The Grandissimes is structured around a series of conflicts, not all of which are satisfactorily resolved. Conflicts exist between families (the Grandissimes and the De Grapions), between members of the same family (Honoré and Agricola, Agricola and Sylvestre), between races (Honoré and Honoré f.m.c., Agricola and Palmyre), and between nationalities (the Creoles and the Americans). Into this world of struggle appears Joseph Frowenfeld, the well-meaning, studious and naive intruder who attempts to assume the role of mediator and finds himself involved in conflicts of his own. On a thematic level, these conflicts become rich—between democracy and aristocracy, the old and the new, the North and the South, American and European values, justice and racism, pride and love, vengeance and forgiveness, innocence and experience, and the list could go on.

As one chapter title indicates, the most difficult conflicts of all are the "Wars within the Breast" (p. 129). Most of the characters are forced to struggle with contradictory feelings, to question long-held attitudes and beliefs, to redefine themselves and their relationships with others. They emerge from this process of questioning and self-examination either changed or destroyed. Honoré must decide whether loyalty to family tradition or to moral conviction is to guide him. Although he succeeds in making the right decision, Honoré f.m.c. and the black characters are not able to redefine themselves in terms of the new society that is created. When the f.m.c. asserts "Ah ham nod a slev," Frowenfeld responds: "Are you certain of that?" (p. 195). One of the questions Cable is concerned with is: what does it mean to be free? And he knew that the Emancipation Proclamation was not a sufficient answer, for, as Frowenfeld says, "there is a slavery that no legislation can abolish,—the slavery of caste. That, like all the slaveries on earth, is a double bondage. And what a bondage it is which compels a community, in order to preserve its established tyrannies, to walk behind the rest of the intelligent world!" (p. 143). Neither whites nor blacks could be fully free until the issues of racism and caste had been confronted and overcome.

The Grandissimes is a book filled with questions. Frowenfeld spends much of his time seeking the answer to questions. Some of the chapter titles underscore the novel's concern with asking basic questions: "And Who Is My Neighbor?" (p. 14) and "Fo' Wad You Cryne?"

(p. 212). Sometimes, however, the questions are implicit. When Frowenfeld asserts that he is an American, Agricola replies: "You are not. You were merely born in America" (p. 86). The question Cable is raising is one that has preoccupied many of our writers: "what does it mean to be an American?" Cable knew that the Civil War had not answered that question. He knew that the South would not really be American until it adopted the principles of freedom and equality.

The presentation of conflicts and questions gains an allusive richness through the symbolic patterns established by the names of the characters. On the most obvious level, names like Brahmin Mandarin de Grandissime suggest a family pride based on antiquated and foreign systems of caste. As the head of the family, Honoré must redefine the term "honor" so that it stands for moral principles and not family pride. The feud between the families is underscored by military allusions: a Fusilier is a soldier armed with a flintlock musket and De Grapion suggests "grape," a word referring to a kind of ammunition. However, Aurora and Clotilde now have the surname, Nancanou, which suggests "unknown," and is therefore appropriate for two characters who create an aura of mystery.

The names often point to the racial conflicts. Dr. Keene's observations on race are anything but keen, as his debate with Clemence establishes. Clemence, of course, meets with no clemency. Bras-Coupé's name explicitly points to the maiming effects of slavery, but the name may have been partially inspired by Cable's knowledge of an unsuccessful slave revolt at Pointe Coupée in 1795, which would be close to the time of Bras-Coupé's arrival in Louisiana.[13] The meaning of Palmyre would have been familiar to nineteenth-century readers who would have known the Syrian city's history either from Gibbon's *Decline and Fall of the Roman Empire,* or William Ware's bestseller, *Zenobia or the Fall of Palmyra* (1837), or one of the travel books of the time. Under the leadership of the Queen Zenobia, Palmyra attempted an unsuccessful revolt against Aurelian and the Roman Empire. Palmyre is therefore an appropriate name for a woman engaged in futile rebellion against more powerful forces.

Cable seems to have selected the name, Joseph Frowenfield, with care. He knew the Bible extremely well and certainly knew of the old testament Joseph, the "dreamer" who is sent into a strange land and prospers until he is falsely accused of an illicit sexual involvement (See Gen. 37, 39–41). The evidence against Joseph is a garment that is left behind when he hastily flees, which corresponds to the hat Frowenfeld leaves. Although all the details do not match, this would not be the first time that a writer used the name Joseph to refer to his naive hero, as the reader of Fielding's *Joseph Andrews* knows. The most important parallel is that Joseph's salvation stems from his ability to be of service to the Egyptians as an interpreter of dreams, just as Frowenfeld becomes the interpreter of the Creoles' dreams. Given the German origin, the name, Frowenfeld, suggests *woman's field* (*frau* and *feld*). Such an interpretation finds support in the passage in which Palmyre is soothed by "his womanly touch, his commanding gentleness, his easy despatch" (p. 135). As the representative of spiritual and moral forces working for peace and civilization, Frowenfeld clearly possesses qualities that the nineteenth century thought of as belonging to the woman's field of endeavor.

Cable's failure to give life to Joseph Frowenfeld is probably the single greatest weakness in the novel. Several critics have reminded us that Frowenfeld is not simply Cable's spokesman but a naive young man who must learn to cope with a complex world.[14] Cable rejects the plantation myth's belief that any Northerner who actually saw the South would be converted to its customs, but he also shows that Northern principles cannot easily convert the South. The problem is not that Frowenfeld is too simple a character, but that Cable is trying to do too much with him. His "large philosophy" sounds ridiculous "in a little parlor" (p. 143). Although, as Clotilde suggests, Frowenfeld is innocent of everything (p. 213), he possesses "that frankness and ardent zeal for truth which had enlisted the early friendship of Doctor Keene, amused and attracted Honoré Grandissime, won the confidence of the f.m.c., and tamed the fiery distrust and enmity of Palmyre" (p. 141). The novel is based not only on his attempt to understand Creole society, but on the ways the Creoles understand and misunderstand him. In fact, the Creoles treat him as though he possesses some kind of magical power. Agricola seems to believe that Frowenfeld will vindicate the Creole cause. Honoré f.m.c. and Palmyre each unsuccessfully turns to him for love potions, and Aurora goes to him for basil which will bring money into her house.

Frowenfeld's interaction with the Creoles is too complex to fit into any simple scheme. In spite of his virtues, he has to depend on the aid of others, and even with their help, he is only partially successful. He spurs Honoré to action, and Honoré teaches him to temper his zeal with caution. The growth of these two characters is paralleled by that of Raoul Innerarity, who begins as a dilettante and a bumbler but becomes a businessman, husband, and peacemaker. The novel presents the growth of these characters, and the marriages between Honoré and Aurora and between Frowenfeld and Clotilde suggest both the reconciliation of the feuding families and of the North and the South. Nevertheless, there is much that remains unresolved.

With Raoul's help, Frowenfeld can stop Agricola's duel with Sylvestre, but Agricola, although softened, does not abandon his old prejudices; he provokes his own death at the hands of the f.m.c., and dies like an old Confederate, confused and uncertain, but proclaiming his loyalties to his sovereign state. None of the characters can prevent the horrible and violent death of Clemence. Frowenfeld and Honoré find love, but Dr. Keene, Palmyre, and the f.m.c. do not. Frowenfeld can help heal the bullet wound in Palmyre's breast, but not the wounds in her heart. Frowenfeld and Honoré can prevent the f.m.c.'s first attempt to drown himself, but not his second one.

At one point, Frowenfeld says that "the truth only is incredible" (p. 208). But it was the truth of history to which Cable remained faithful. Cable understood how much Reconstruction had resolved and how much it had failed to resolve. The reconciliation of the North and the South had been achieved, but the attempt to reconcile the races ended, as Newton Arvin points out, in "failure and tragedy."[15] The name, *Grandissime Brothers*, turns out to be merely a linguistic victory, as the Emancipation Proclamation was. Instead of becoming truly free, the f.m.c. and Palmyre are forced to flee into exile and remain unredeemed by love. The issues raised in *The Grandissimes* were not resolved in 1803–04 or in 1880; they have not yet been resolved today. Perhaps it is not accidental that the novel ends with an ironic chapter, entitled "No!" (p. 336).

Cable went on to devote many years of his life to saying "no" to racism and the lies of the plantation myth. In doing so, he became, as H.H. Boyesen predicted, the "founder of a new school" of Southern writing, writing committed to a complex probing of the moral issues of both the past and the present.[16]

NOTES

[1]See *The Writer in the South* (Athens: Univ. of Georgia Press, 1972) and Rubin's essay, "Southern Local Color and the Black Man," *Southern Review*, 6 (Autumn 1970), 1011–30. For a discussion of black figures in antebellum American literature and of the plantation myth, see Jean Fagin Yellin, *The Intricate Knot* (New York: New York Univ. Press, 1972).

[2]"The South as a Field for Fiction," *Forum*, 6 (1886), 405. For a fuller account of postbellum fiction, see Jay Martin, *Harvests of Change* (Englewood Cliffs, N.J.: Prentice-Hall, 1967).

[3]*George W. Cable: The Life and Times of a Southern Heretic* (New York: Pegasus, 1969), p. 78. All biographical information on Cable in this essay comes from Arlin Turner, *George W. Cable: A Biography* (Durham: Duke Univ. Press, 1956).

[4]The most perceptive comments on Cable's writings may be found in the works by Rubin, Martin, and Turner cited earlier and in Newton Arvin, Introduction, *The Grandissimes* (New York: Hill and Wang, 1957), pp. v–xi; Richard Chase, *The American Novel and Its Tradition* (Garden City, N.Y.: Doubleday, 1957), pp. 167–76.; Richard Bozman Eaton, "George W. Cable and the Historical Romance," *The Southern Literary Journal*, 8 (Fall 1975), 82–94; John Cleman, "The Art of Local Color in George W. Cable's *The Grandissimes*," *American Literature*, 47 (November 1975), 396–410; and Robert O. Stephens, "Cable's *The Grandissimes* and the Comedy of Manners," *American Literature*, 51 (January 1980), 507–19.

[5]Quoted in Arlin Turner, "A Novelist Discovers a Novelist: The Correspondence of H. H. Boyesen and George W. Cable," *Western Humanities Review*, 5 (Autumn 1951), 346–47.

[6]"A Novelist Discovers a Novelist," 347.

[7]Quoted in Philip Butcher, "Cable to Boyesen on *The Grandissimes*," *American Literature*, 40 (November 1968), 393.

[8]"After-Thoughts of a Story-Teller," *North American Review*, 158 (Jan. 1894), 17.

[9]"A Novelist Discovers a Novelist," p. 358.

[10]*The Grandissimes* (New York: Hill and Wang, 1957), p. 96. All further quotations from *The Grandissimes* are from this edition and will be cited parenthetically in my text.

[11]Excerpt from Cable's diary quoted in Arvin, p. viii.

[12]*The Creoles of Louisiana* (New York: Charles Scribner's Sons, 1889), p. 51.

[13]*The Creoles of Louisiana*, p. 125.

[14]See Stephens' article and Donald Ringe, "The 'Double Center': Character and Meaning in Cable's Early Novels," *Studies in the Novel*, 5 (Spring 1973), 52–62.

[15]Arvin, p. xi.

[16]"A Novelist Discovers a Novelist," p. 368.

The Grandissimes and the French Quarter

Text by W. KENNETH HOLDITCH
Photographs by DRAYTON HAMILTON

As anyone familiar with the major works of George Washington Cable
knows, the French Quarter of New Orleans is central to his novels and
stories, serving often not only as setting but also as inspiration and
symbol. The Quarter was, for Cable, that other world, different from
the world of his uptown upbringing, from his Calvinistic training and
inclinations; different from the rest of the Protestant South; a place
distinct in its atmosphere, its attitudes, its morality, and in the inten-
sity of living. Surely the way in which the young Cable looked at the
old city must have been something like the response of Henry Sutpen
as envisioned by Mr. Compson: "I can imagine him, with his puritan
heritage—that heritage peculiarly Anglo-Saxon—of fierce proud mys-
ticism and that ability to be ashamed of ignorance and inexperience,
in that city foreign and paradoxical, with its atmosphere at once fatal
and languorous, at once feminine and steel-hard—a place whose
denizens had created their All-Powerful and His supporting
hierarchy-chorus of beautiful saints and handsome angels in the
image of their houses and personal ornaments and voluptuous lives
. . . ."[1] Cable, however, unlike Henry, was not to remain ignorant of
that "place created for and by voluptuousness, the abashless and
unabashed senses";[2] his attitude early and late is expressive of an
ambivalent response to the exotic area and its "denizens."

That Cable retained a moralistic view of the activities, virtuous or
vicious, of the Creoles—very similar, by the way, to that expressed by
W. C. C. Claiborne when he first came to New Orleans in the opening
years of the nineteenth century to serve as governor of the new
American territory—is evident from his works. But equally evident is
the fact that he was attracted to it, inspired by it, despite (or perhaps
even to some extent because of) the "voluptuousness." It was, surely,

on the one hand a symbol of that other way of life, which he with his scruples found distasteful, representing as it did luxury and wealth built on slavery, a system that appalled not only Cable and his protagonist Joseph Frowenfeld, but Governor Claiborne as well.

When one considers the French Quarter in relation to *The Grandissimes*, of course, there are actually three quite distinct time levels to be recognized. There is the Vieux Carré of a century ago, the time of the writing of *The Grandissimes*, the area, in other words, as Cable himself knew it. Equally important is the Quarter as it was—or as the author with the aid of research and his fertile imagination portrayed it as having been—in 1803 and 1804, the time of the cession of the colony to the United States. Finally, there is the Quarter today, a far cry from the French city of almost two hundred years ago, considerably altered from the early productive years of Cable, although of course the fact of its recognition within this century as an invaluable and irreplaceable historical area has contributed to its having been preserved to a greater extent than many other American cities or towns.

The following photographs of Cable's home and of the modern Quarter are offered as a tribute to Cable's art in his greatest novel, *The Grandissimes*. Further, they constitute an attempt to give the reader unfamiliar with the area some sense of what the Quarter is now like and at least a hint of the region as Cable knew it and wrote about it. Imagine the "little, hybrid city of 'Nouvelle Orleans' " as the Frowenfeld family first saw it that day in 1803:

> There was the cathedral, and standing beside it, like Sancho beside Don Quixote, the squat hall of the Cabildo with the calabozo in the rear. There were the forts, the military bakery, the hospitals, the plaza, the Almonaster stores, and the busy rue Toulouse; and, for the rest of the town, a pleasant confusion of green tree-tops, red and gray roofs, and glimpses of white or yellow wall, spreading back a few hundred yards behind the cathedral, and tapering into a single rank of gardened and belvedered villas, that studded either horn of the river's crescent with a style of home than which there is probably nothing in the world more maternally home-like.[3]

"Tho' much is taken, much abides," and the reader familiar with the Vieux Carré will recognize from Cable's descriptions certain details of the area as it exists even now. There are buildings, of course, that were standing when the Frowenfelds set foot on the levee at Place d'Armes, including among others the Ursuline convent and "Madame John's

The George Washington Cable Home
1313 Eighth Street

"Frowenfeld's Corner"

The Place d'Armes

The Daniel Clark House
823 Royal

Congo Square

*The Veau-qui-tete Restaurant
(The Suckling Calf)*

Exchange Alley

Maspero's

The Skyscraper

Chartres Street

Legacy," the house which Cable named, made famous, and probably as a result of that name and fame saved in recent years from "demolition by neglect." With a fraction of the imagination which Cable himself so amply possessed, one may be able to envision beneath the inescapable signs of modernization and "progress" the exotic milieu in which the larger-than-life characters of *The Grandissimes* moved.

The George Washington Cable Home, 1313 Eighth Street. In 1876 Cable bought two lots on Eighth Street in uptown New Orleans, a couple of miles from the French Quarter but near the area of his birth, and built a house on them, completed in 1878. It was here that he lived with his wife and children until their move to the East, here that his son George died of yellow fever, here that the famous gathering of Cable, Mark Twain and Joel Chandler Harris occurred in April 1882, here that *The Grandissimes* was written. The house is of a typical Louisiana design, a Greek Revival structure with the dwelling area raised one floor above ground level for the purpose, ironical in view of the son's death, of warding off yellow fever.

"Frowenfeld's Corner." Cable describes Joseph's apothecary shop as "a small, single-story building in the rue Royale,—corner of Conti. . . ." (p. 41) The combination shop and residence, a typical arrangement in the Quarter until recent decades, no longer stands on the corner, now occupied by the American Legion Hall, the Wildlife and Fisheries Building, and two antique shops in buildings which despite their ancient vintage do not match the author's description. As "Frowenfeld's corner," the shop served as a gathering place for Americans and some Creoles (Agricola Fusilier, for instance) until it was demolished by a mob.

The Place d'Armes. Designed in 1720 by Bienville, the square, bounded by Decatur, St. Peter, Chartres, and St. Ann Streets, was originally a parade ground for the militia. In the early 1800s, the time of the novel, it was the center of life in the Vieux Carre and has remained so to the present time. Now known as Jackson Square in honor of the "savior" of New Orleans, the Place d'Armes in early days was surrounded by the official buildings of church and state and by warehouses. On Chartres Street, the cathedral stands today as it has since its construction in 1852, between the older Cabildo (the seat of government) and the Presbytere (the seat of ecclesiastical power).

Where once the warehouses stood on St. Ann and St. Peter now stand the upper and lower Pontalba buildings, constructed in 1849–1850. Cable describes the Place d'Armes in Chapter 15 as the gathering place on warm, balmy days of every type New Orleanian, from Honoré Grandissime and Governor Claiborne on one end of the social scale to Clemence, the seller of rice cakes, on the other. "Before the view lies the Place d'Armes in its greenbreasted uniform of new spring grass crossed diagonally with white shell walks for facings, and dotted with the *élite* of the city for decorations. Over the line of shade-trees which marks its farther boundary, the white-topped twin turrets of St. Louis Cathedral look across it and beyond . . . and out upon the Mississippi. . . ." (p. 78).

The Daniel Clark House, 823 Royal. Daniel Clark, who came to New Orleans in 1786 and made a fortune in the import business, was American consul in the city during the last years of Spanish rule. Several years after his death in 1813, Myra Clark Gaines instituted one of the most involved and protracted litigations in the history of American jurisprudence to prove herself the legitimate daughter and heir to Clark's fortune. Cable comments on the case in *The Grandissimes* when he places the wealthy New Orleanian among the throng taking the air in the Place d'Armes: "There was young Daniel Clark, already beginning to amass those riches which an age of litigation has not to this day consumed; it was he whom the French colonial prefect, Laussat, in a late letter to France, had extolled as a man whose 'talents for intrigue were carried to a rare degree of excellence' " (p. 79).

Congo Square. To this small park area on Rampart Street (then literally the ramparts of the city), Quarter residents at the time of the novel's action (and indeed up until the Civil War) would bring their slaves on Sunday afternoons for their weekly fellowship and recreation. It is here that Bras-Coupé was captured shortly before his death. Cable, who was intrigued by the music of the slaves, examined these gatherings and the pastimes of the blacks in two essays, "The Dance in 'Place Congo,' " and "Creole Slave Songs." His description of these festivities in *The Grandissimes* recreates imaginatively what the limited pleasures of these people in bondage must have been like.

> It was on a Sabbath afternoon that a band of Choctaws having just played a game of racquette behind the city and a similar game being about to end

between the white champions of two rival faubourgs, the beating of tom-toms, rattling of mules' jawbones and sounding of wooden horns drew the populace across the fields to a spot whose present name of Congo Square still preserves a reminder of its old barbaric pastimes. On a grassy plain under the ramparts, the performers of these hideous discords sat upon the ground facing each other, and in their midst the dancers danced. They gyrated in couples, a few at a time, throwing their bodies into the most startling attitudes and the wildest contortions, while the whole company of black lookers-on, incited by the tones of the weird music and the violent posturing of the dancers, swayed and writhed in passionate sympathy, beating their breasts, palms and thighs in time with the bones and drums, and at frequent intervals lifting, in that wild African unison no more to be described than forgotten, the unutterable songs of Babouille and Counjaille dances, with their ejaculatory burdens of "*Aie! Aie! Voudoo Magnan!*" and "*Aie Calinda. Dancé Calinda!*" (p. 189)

Today the square has been engulfed by Louis Armstrong Park, a multi-million-dollar project instituted by a former mayor which has converted the last remnants of the historic spot and surrounding area into an ultra-modern development of steel and concrete.

The Veau-qui-tête Restaurant (The Suckling Calf). The building which now houses Le Petit Theatre and occupies the corner of St. Peter and Chartres opposite the upper Pontalba building and the Cabildo is surely the one which Cable describes as the location of this gathering place for Creole gentlemen. The original structure was begun in 1789; in the nineteenth century it contained a succession of restaurants and bars; and in 1962, it was rebuilt to house the theater organization. It is here that Frowenfeld first goes seeking Sylvestre Grandissime in the hope of preventing the impending duel between Sylvestre and Agricola.

The Veau-qui-tête restaurant occupied the whole ground floor of a small, low, two-story, tile-roofed, brick-and-stucco building which still stands on the corner of Chartres and St. Peter streets, in company with the well-preserved old Cabildo and the young Cathedral, reminding one of the shabby and swarthy Creoles whom we sometimes see helping better kept kinsmen to murder time on the banquettes of the old French Quarter. It was a favorite rendezvous of the higher classes, convenient to the court-rooms and municipal bureaus. There you found the choicest legal and political gossips, with the best the market afforded of meat and drink. (p. 237)

Exchange Alley. Once stretching through the four blocks from Canal Street to St. Louis, between Royal and Chartres, the alley was shortened by one block in 1910 by the building of the courthouse (now the

Wildlife and Fisheries Building) on the square bounded by Royal, St. Louis, Chartres and Conti Streets. Cable noted its proximity to the early banks and exchanges of the city when he described it as "once *Passage de la Bourse*" which "led down (as it now does to the State House—late St. Louis Hotel)" to Maspero's (p. 239). The alley has within recent years been the object of considerable renovation after decades of neglect.

Maspero's. Currently a popular restaurant at the corner of Chartres and St. Louis, Maspero's occupies a fascinating old building constructed in 1788, after the great New Orleans fire which had begun in the adjacent block. Cable seemed uncertain of the address, but locates the general vicinity, and his authorial doubt as to the exact age of the establishment attests to the romantic confusion that clouds much history of the city. The Maspero's Cable described was "an establishment which seems to have served for a long term of years as a sort of merchants' and auctioneers' coffee-house, with a minimum of china and a maximum of glass: Maspero's—certainly Maspero's as far back as 1810, and, we believe, Maspero's the day the apothecary entered it, March 9, 1804. It was a livelier spot than the Veau-qui-tête; it was to that what commerce is to litigation, what standing and quaffing is to sitting and sipping. Whenever the public mind approached that sad state of public sentiment in which sanctity signs politicians' memorials and chivalry breaks into the gun-shops, a good place to feel the thump of the machinery was in Maspero's" (p. 239).

The Skyscraper. This oddly-shaped building with its third-floor oval room stands on the corner of Royal and St. Peter Streets. It served Cable well, of course, in his first published story, " 'Sieur George," and his mention of it in *The Grandissimes* suggests that he felt a sentimental attachment for it. The passage occurs in a conversation between Honoré Grandissime and an unnamed client:

> "I understand that Nicholas Girod is proposing to erect a four-story brick building on the corner of Royale and St. Pierre. Do you think it practicable? Do you think our soil will support such a structure?"
> "Pitot thinks it will. Boré says it is perfectly feasible." (p. 247)

Cable's reference to three men prominent in the history of the city, a practice he often employs in the novel, adds an air of authenticity to his work. The reader may be amused to speculate what those three

Creoles and Cable himself might think if they could see the real skyscrapers in New Orleans' Central Business District in 1980.

Chartres Street. In his discussion of the new building in which Joseph opens his apothecary shop after vandals have destroyed "Frowenfeld's Corner," Cable comments on that unique blending of residences and businesses which marks the Vieux Carré even today. "In those days, as still in the old French Quarter, it was not uncommon for persons, even of wealth, to make their homes over stores, and buildings were constructed with a view to their partition in this way. Hence, in Chartres and Decatur streets, to-day—and in the cross-streets between, so many store-buildings with balconies, dormer windows, and sometimes even belvederes" (p. 285). This contemporary view of Chartres, looking away from Canal, toward the cathedral, exhibits the type structure which Cable described.

In several ways, the French Quarter, beyond the surface uniqueness which made it eminently suitable for an author of the local color school, is important in the fiction of Cable; and a knowledge of the place is a significant aid to the understanding of that fiction. If he were alive today, Cable would be, as many lovers of the city are, disturbed by the commercialism that has spread like a plague over the surface of much of the Quarter. The cheap "boutiques" and burlesque houses and outlets for shoddy garments imprinted with scatalogical slogans would surely not only have pained but also offended the writer who could recreate so powerfully the musty, ancient air of the region's streets and shops and houses. Subsequent generations, even those who have never read him, are heirs to a vision of the atmosphere and life of the Quarter that owe more to Cable's writing than to any other source.

NOTES

[1]William Faulkner, *Absalom, Absalom!* (New York: Random House, 1936), pp. 108–09.

[2]Faulkner, p. 114.

[3]*The Grandissimes* (New York: Hill and Wang, 1957), p. 11. Subsequent references to this volume will be indicated by page numbers in parentheses after citations.

Humor in Cable's *The Grandissimes*

WILLIAM BEDFORD CLARK

At the end of May 1865, George Washington Cable returned to New Orleans wearing the remnants of his Confederate uniform. He found a much needed job as messenger for a tobacco house—something of a comedown for a young man who had clerked for General Forrest during the war—and he was dispatched on one occasion to the headquarters of the occupying Union army. The commanding Officer, General Banks, was ruffled to see Cable in his tattered gray, and reminded the errand boy that he was breaking the law to appear in public in the uniform of the defeated South. Cable's reply has become legendary: "Yes, sir, I know that, sir. But I remember an older law which I am bound to regard, which forbids a man to appear without any clothes at all, sir."[1] Arlin Turner seems to suggest that Cable's response may have been embellished a bit by his imagination over the years,[2] but whether or not that is the case Cable's famous exchange with Banks is highly suggestive. It not only reminds us of Cable's ready wit, a characteristic noted frequently by his contemporaries, but, taken in the context of the South's defeat and the bleak prospects Cable and his family faced in the wake of surrender, it offers us insight into Cable's peculiar brand of humor. Laughter played a significant role in Cable's life, and in his writings. At times, it seems to have furnished him with a buffer against too close an involvement with painful realities. Perhaps nowhere is the range of Cable's comic sense more in evidence than in his first and best novel, *The Grandissimes*, and yet the critics, in their concern for the serious social commentary in that book, have tended to neglect the fact that humor, at times tinged with horror, is its dominant mode.

In the broadest sense, the very structure of Cable's novel follows a conventionally "comic" pattern. The lovers, Honoré Grandissime and

51

Aurora Nancanou, come together in spite of all the family obstacles and social complications that stand in their way, and the book ends with the promise of their wedding and that of the pharmacist Frowenfeld and Aurora's daughter Clotilde, representatives of a new generation. The witty repartee of the opening chapter, which clearly owes much to the traditional comedy of manners, finds its congenial complement in the novel's final scene, in which Aurora, laughing through her tears, teasingly accepts Honoré's proposal of marriage. To be sure, sandwiched between these two chapters there is suffering, disease, cruelty, and death enough to furnish the raw materials for a full scale tragedy, and Cable is unquestionably a master of nineteenth-century fictive *pathos*, playing sentiment and social criticism against one another for all they are worth. Still, even these darker events are frequently punctuated with laughter. It is the comic muse that ultimately presides over *The Grandissimes* as a whole, and an analysis of the way in which humor functions in the novel is essential to a fuller understanding of Cable's achievement.

Viewed in isolation, much of the humor in *The Grandissimes* seems gratuitous, yet Cable did not consider it so. In 1900, looking back over his career, Cable reiterated his opinion that the first duty of fiction was to be entertaining: "The more nobly it amuses, or rather the more nobly amusing it is, the higher does it rise in greatness and in profitableness."[3] A remark that Honoré makes to Frowenfeld in the course of the novel contains an implicit corollary to this same idea. Concerned by the hostility and resentment arising from the younger man's blunt criticism of slavery and caste, Honoré reminds the pharmacist that he would never "make pills with eight corners."[4] Pills are round to facilitate swallowing them, Honoré continues, and Frowenfeld would do well to apply that principle to the doctrines he prescribes to cure Louisiana's social ills. Cable had used a different figure to express the same basic notion in a letter to H.H. Boyesen written in 1878, during *The Grandissimes*' lengthy gestation period: ". . . novels ought to have a moral effect; they ought to nourish the soul as viands do the body; maybe you don't believe it but I believe it. However, I don't propose to permit any novelist . . . to hold me on his lap and spoon his morals down me to the limits of distention!"[5] A healthy dash of humor is one way to render a novel's moral nourishment more palatable, and this strategy accounts for the presence in *The Grandissimes* of a character like Raoul Innerarity, the would-be artist who, upon realizing his "talent," determines to "never . . . do anoder lick o' work" as long as he lives (p. 115). It also accounts, in part at least, for Cable's exploitation of the comic potential of the Creole and black dialects and his frequent play upon words, as illustrated by the scene in which the reader is told how Aurora's ancestor, a Huguenot girl, resists the pressure to take a husband and convert to Catholicism: " . . . she would neither marry nor pray to Mary" (p. 26). These effects are in keeping with the local color tradition in which *The Grandissimes* is, as John Cleman reminds us, firmly rooted,[6] and the witty authorial tone Cable adopts in many passages clearly shares much in common with the characteristic "voices" of Bret Harte and Joel Chandler Harris in stories like "The Outcasts of Poker Flat" and "Free Joe and the Rest of the World," fiction that likewise sweetens an otherwise bitter dose of morality with a measure of humor and "tearful comedy."

However, in spite of Cable's professed awareness of the novelist's duty to amuse while he instructs, it would be a serious mistake to dismiss the pervasive humor of *The Grandissimes* as little more than attractive packaging for Cable's serious social message, or to regard it merely as skillfully-paced comic relief. Laughter plays a remarkably complex role in the novel. Indeed, it has its darker implications, for Cable's comic vision is based upon some decidedly tough-minded insights into the way of the world. In this regard, an analysis of the laughter of two characters in particular, Dr. Keene and Clemence the cake vendor, is revealing.

Dr. Keene is a cultivated wag who expends his barbed wit upon whatever targets are available. Amid the confusion following the cession of Louisiana to the United States, there is much indecision among influential New Orleanians as to which faction they had best support. Dr. Keene's reaction is characteristic: "One of the things I pity most in this vain world . . . is a hive of patriots who don't know where to swarm" (p. 46). His bedside manner with Frowenfeld, who is the sole member of his family to survive the yellow fever, is also typical: "I have taken a heap of trouble to keep you alive, and if you should relapse now and give us the slip, it would be a deal of good physic wasted; so keep in the house" (p. 13). Likewise, when Dr.

Keene examines the wound Agricola Fusilier suffers in Palmyre's attempt to assassinate him, he pronounces it "only a safe and comfortable gash that will keep you in-doors a while . . ." (pp. 98–99). Yet, Cable tells us that Dr. Keene is a man who finds it hard to deal with his feelings and, especially, with his affection for others (p. 14). He faces Frowenfeld across a chess board as a way of establishing a formal distance between himself and his young friend, and his gruff, at times cynical, humor is likewise a way of distancing himself from too close an involvement with his own emotions. After all, Dr. Keene not only suffers the pangs of unrequited love, he suffers from terminal consumption as well. Returning to the city after an unsuccessful attempt at recuperation, the doctor is told by Raoul that he is "lookingue fine," a remark to which he responds with a "smile of bitter humor" (p. 274). Soon afterward, he resumes his care of yellow fever victims, remarking to himself that it will be "a sort of decent suicide without the element of pusillanimity" (p. 296), and when Honoré implies that he has a bad case of love-sickness, Dr. Keene answers with ominous irony, "It isn't going to kill me" (p. 301). Dr. Keene's humor, then, is colored by suffering and an awareness of impending doom.

Like Dr. Keene, Clemence, the black *marchande des calas,* is notorious for her stinging wit. She is more than a match for the doctor in one-on-one repartee, and the satiric lyrics of her songs reveal a sense of humor that is not altogether good natured. It is Clemence who leads the other slaves in the Calinda dance and "that well-known song of derision, in whose ever multiplying stanzas the helpless satire of a feeble race still continues to celebrate the personal failings of each newly prominent figure among the dominant caste" (p. 95). Clemence may be "a constant singer and laugher," but Cable makes it clear that her heritage, savagery and deprivation in the Old World and bondage in the New, has left her with only "the cinders of human feelings" (p. 251). In this respect, she resembles two of Mark Twain's black characters, Aunt Rachel in the 1874 sketch "A True Story" and the mulatto Roxana in *Pudd'nhead Wilson,* who is capable of the kind of laughter reserved for "the happy angels in heaven and the bruised and broken black slave on earth."[7] Twain's phrase fits Clemence's condition admirably, for hers is the laughter of one with little to lose in the world, a fact that, ironically enough, enables her to comment upon the tragic absurdities of her society from something not unlike a transcendent perspective. She thus becomes the perfect spokesperson for Cable's satiric assault upon racial bigotry in the South. This is particularly apparent in the sarcasm with which she concludes an argument with Dr. Keene: " . . . white folks is werry kine. Dey wants us to b'lieb we happy—dey *wants to b'lieb* we is. W'y, you know, dey 'bleeged to b'lieb it—fo' dey own cyumfut. 'Tis de sem weh wid de preache's; dey buil' we ow own sep'ate meet'n-houses; dey b'leebs us lak it de bess, an' dey *knows* dey lak it de bess" (pp. 250–251).

At this point, Cable is quick to add that the laughter at this observation was largely Clemence's own. There is nothing "laughable," he asserts, in the sight of "the comfortable fractions of Christian communities . . . striving, with sincere, pious, well-meant, criminal benevolence, to make their poor brethren contented with the ditch" (p. 251). But even in this rather heavy-handed example of authorial intrusion, Cable, in coupling the terms "criminal" and "benevolence," is himself engaging in a kind of grim humor. In fact, *The Grandissimes* abounds in passages in which Cable brings this same humor to bear on the issues which he takes most seriously. I suggest that such humor was for Cable, as for Dr. Keene and Clemence, a kind of "defensive" mechanism, one which allowed him to distance himself from the action and characters of his novel in order to deal with them more effectively.

The opening paragraph of Chapter 4 is typical of the detached comic stance Cable adopts throughout the novel, and it is therefore worth quoting in full:

> In the year 1673, and in the royal hovel of a Tchoupitoulas village not far removed from that "Buffalo's Grazing-ground," now better known as New Orleans, was born Lufki-Humma, otherwise Red Clay. The mother of Red Clay was a princess by birth as well as by marriage. For the father, with that devotion to his people's interests, presumably common to rulers, had ten moons before ventured northward into the territory of the proud and exclusive Natchez nation, and had so prevailed with—so outsmoked—their "Great Sun," as to find himself, as he finally knocked the ashes from his successful calumet, possessor of a wife whose pedigree included a long line of royal mothers,—fathers being of little account in Natchez heraldry, extending back beyond the Mexican origin of her nation, and disappearing

only in the effulgence of her great original, the orb of day himself. As to Red
Clay's paternal ancestry, we must content ourselves with the fact that the
father was not only the diplomat we have already found him, but a chief of
considerable eminence; that is to say, of seven feet stature. (p. 17)

Cable's humor here, as elsewhere, is functional, serving to burlesque
Creole pretensions regarding distinguished ancestors, but what is
more remarkable is the way in which he brings the same urbane
condescension to bear on aspects of Louisiana life that he clearly does
not find so amusing—dueling for example. Here is his two-line description of the duel that ends the career of Georges De Grapion:
"Bang! bang!/Alas, Madame De Grapion!" (p. 28). Indeed, the touchy
theme of miscegenation, which through the presence of Palmyre
Philosophe and Honoré, f.m.c., underscores the wrongs growing out
of slavery and caste, is itself on occasion treated in much the same
cavalier fashion, as when Cable remarks how the Grandissimes have
kept their bloodline "lily-white" as far as marriage is concerned: "as to
less responsible entanglements, why, of course—" (p. 22). Similarly,
in a misguided attempt to establish the primacy of his family ties,
Raoul at one point claims that "De mose of de Creole families is not so
hold as plenty of my yallah kinfolks!" (p. 119). Even the tragic account
of the career of Bras-Coupé, Cable's emblematic assertion of "the
truth that all Slavery is maiming" (p. 171), is fraught with a kind of
bitter humor.

The African prince arrives in the New World aboard the "good
schooner *Egalité*" (a nice irony), but many of his fellows do not
survive the passage: "Part of the living merchandise failed to keep;
the weather was rough, the cargo large, the vessel small. However, the
captain discovered there was room over the side, and there—all flesh
is grass—from time to time during the voyage he jettisoned the un-
merchantable" (p. 169). This is black humor indeed, but there is more.
Bras-Coupé's first impressions of New Orleans include a glimpse of "a
most inviting jail, convenient to the cathedral," and he soon finds
himself down river at La Renaissance plantation where a number of
"agreeable surprises" await him (p. 170). Cable treats the African's
initial culture shock with the condescending amusement we have
noted earlier, and Bras-Coupé's first flight toward freedom is re-
counted with a comic exaggeration reminiscent of the humor of the

Old Southwest. The fleeing Bras-Coupé is finally brought down by a ball from the overseer's pistol: "It had struck him in the forehead, and running around the skull in search of a penetrable spot, tradition—which sometimes jests—says came out despairingly, exactly where it had entered." We are told that all the damage was easily remedied, except in the case of the slave driver Bras-Coupé brained with a hoe, "—for the driver," Cable states matter-of-factly, "died" (p. 172).

The story of Bras-Coupé continues in much the same spirit up to the point where his wedding to Palmyre—arranged by the whites as an explicit comic parallel to the marriage of Honoré's sister and the African's Spanish master—is imminent. Here the narrative reaches a comic climax of sorts, only to have the narrative tone shift from humorous to horrific. Having painted his body in tribal fashion, Bras-Coupé initially refuses to dress for the ceremony, but he finally appears in "ridiculous red and blue regimentals, but with a look of savage dignity . . . that keeps every one from laughing" (p. 178). Outside, a violent thunderstorm is brewing, and it signals the coming of an equally violent melodrama inside the Grandissime mansion, when the African, drunk and sensing betrayal on the part of the whites, strikes the Spaniard and strikes out for the swamps, setting in motion the sequence of events which blights the fates of all concerned.

This shift from humor to high melodrama has its lesser analogues elsewhere in the novel. Early on, there is a bit of slapstick which takes a serious turn when Agricola, in the midst of a rhapsody of boasting, stumbles over the purse Aurora has dropped in Frowenfeld's pharmacy. The public ridicule of the "disgraced" Frowenfeld who emerges wounded from Palmyre's house, a ridicule Cable obviously invites the reader to relish, threatens eventually to turn into a riot, and Cable's witty account of the Grandissime *fête* ends with an impending duel between kinsmen. Similarly, Agricola's fatal encounter with Honoré, f.m.c., is preceded by the same kind of *alazon* bluster with which the old man has, unintentionally, made himself laughable throughout the narrative.[8] But the most striking, indeed most shocking, example of Cable's use of this technique comes when he narrates the details surrounding the capture and death of old Clemence.

When Clemence, stealthily carrying the voodou curse of Palmyre to

the house of Agricola, is suddenly caught in a steel trap, she screams
out in pain:

> "*Ah! bon Dieu, bon Dieu!* Quit a-*bi-i-i-i-tin'* me! Oh! Lawd 'a' mussy!
> Ow-ow-ow! lemme go! Dey go'n' to kyetch an' hang me! Oh! an' I hain'
> done nuttin' 'gainst *no*body! Ah! *bon Dieu! ein pov' vié négresse!* Oh!
> Jemimy! I cyan' gid dis yeh t'ing loose—oh! m-m-m-m! An' dey'll tra to mek
> out 't I voudou' Mich-Agricole! An' I didn' had nutt'n' do wid it! Oh Lawd,
> oh, *Lawd,* you'll be mighty good ef you lemme loose! I'm a po' nigga! Oh!
> dey hadn' ought to mek it so *pow'*ful!" (pp. 312–313)

If this torment is somehow *laughable,* and I submit that it is, it is not so
simply because of the fact that it is expressed in dialect, for Clemence's anguish has about it much of the quality of the conventional
"darky" humor we encounter in B'rer Rabbit, where pain is presented
with the unreality of the violence in slapstick. But we are shocked into
realizing the real agony of Clemence's situation by Cable's next observation: "Hands, teeth, the free foot, the writhing body, every combination of available forces failed to spread the savage jaws, though
she strove until hands and mouth were bleeding" (p. 313). Cable
interjects bits of humor throughout his account of Clemence's ordeal,
leading up to that point in the story at which it appears that she will be
spared after all. Sylvestre Grandissime and Raoul interrupt the lynch-
ing, only to allow the scene to become a grotesque game in which the
crippled woman is allowed to run for her life. Cable observes that "It
was so funny to see her scuttling and tripping and stumbling" (p. 323),
until a shot rings out and Clemence dies instantly. Here Cable is
walking a kind of Faulknerian "tightrope between the ridiculous . . .
and the terrible."[9] He is skillfully manipulating the reader's response
to enhance the horror of the episode, and his blend of humor and
horror in his treatment of Clemence's fate is in keeping with a tradition
in Southern literature that begins at least as early as Poe and reaches a
high point in the work of Welty, McCullers, and O'Connor. Cable's
outrage over racial injustice was very real here and in the story of
Bras-Coupé as well,[10] but his outrage is kept in check, at least within
the context of his novel, by a mitigating sense of humor. However
bitter it may be at times, it tempers the author's anger and enables him
to deal with it as a craftsman.

Donald A. Ringe has argued convincingly that the moral center of

The Grandissimes does not reside solely in the pronouncements of the libertarian Frowenfeld, but rather that it emerges out of the dialectical relationship of Frowenfeld and Honoré.[11] It is therefore significant that Frowenfeld's righteous indignation is singularly lacking in a comic sense, while Honoré's condemnation of his society's racial mores is informed by his sense of humor. The criticisms of Frowenfeld serve only to breed resentment among the citizens of New Orleans; it is left to Honoré to take action to dispel at least some of the wrongs of the past. An analysis of Cable's complex use of humor in *The Grandissimes* suggests that he sensed, however consciously, that uncontrolled anger was finally ineffectual in fiction and, more importantly, in life itself. "Keep glad!" he advised his children, "It's the best way of serving God that was ever revealed."[12] In a very real sense, Cable took his own advice—as a writer, a social reformer, and as a man.

NOTES

[1]Lucy Leffingwell Cable Biklé, *George W. Cable: His Life and Letters* (New York: Scribner's, 1928), pp. 24–25.

[2]*George W. Cable: A Biography* (Baton Rouge: Louisiana State Univ. Press, 1966), p. 35.

[3]Cited in Biklé, p. 248.

[4]*The Grandissimes* (New York: Hill and Wang, 1957), p. 153. All subsequent quotations from the novel are from this edition and page numbers will be given parenthetically in the text.

[5]See Turner, p. 81.

[6]"The Art of Local Color in George W. Cable's *The Grandissimes*," *American Literature*, 47 (1975), 396–410.

[7]*Pudd'nhead Wilson*, introd. F.R. Leavis (New York: Grove Press, 1955), p. 144.

[8]Elsewhere I have argued that Cable's "incongruent" portrayal of Agricola is a flaw in his work. See "Cable and the Theme of Miscegenation in *Old Creole Days* and *The Grandissimes*," *Mississippi Quarterly*, 30 (1977), 606–07. In light of my revised understanding of Cable's use of humor in his novel, I no longer hold such an opinion.

[9]See *Faulkner at the University*, ed. Frederick L. Gwynn and Joseph L. Blotner (Charlottesville: Univ. of Virginia Press, 1959), p. 39.

[10]Biklé says that the Bras-Coupé episode grew out of her father's "sheer indignation" over the Black Code (p. 45). Originally entitled "Bibi," it was rejected by a succession of editors, including those at the *Atlantic*, though William Dean Howells would later call the version incorporated in the novel "most powerful." See Louis D. Rubin, Jr., *George W. Cable: The Life and Times of a Southern Heretic* (New York: Pegasus, 1969), p. 98. Although "Bibi" does not survive, it is interesting to speculate on how much of the humor of the revised version was added in an effort to bring the author's indignation under control.

[11]"The 'Double Center': Character and Meaning in Cable's Early Novels," *Studies in the Novel*, 5 (1973), 52–53.

[12]See Biklé, p. xii.

The Free Man of Color in *The Grandissimes* and Works by Harris and Mark Twain

LAWRENCE I. BERKOVE

When Reconstruction ended with the Compromise of 1877, the South advanced in the areas of local government and economic development but regressed in civil rights. Blacks, who had been enfranchised by the federal government, were deprived by the Southern states of most of the substance of the freedom to which they now held legal title. Black freedmen all over the South found their freedom a bitter delusion, and few white allies came forward to offer them support. Among the few who did, however, were the South's three most eminent literary figures: George Washington Cable, Joel Chandler Harris, and Mark Twain. These authors responded immediately to the situation in major works of the 1880s. By their common use of the motif of the f.m.c. (free man of color), they drew an ominous parallel between the tenuous liberties of the black freedman of the post-Reconstruction South and the anomolous condition of the ante-bellum f.m.c.[1] Although their literary settings were in the pre-Civil War South, the three authors metaphorically addressed issues that were contemporaneous. From the point of view afforded them by their use of the motif of the f.m.c., Cable, Harris, and Twain were not only critical of the South but also pessimistic in their prognostications of what was implied by the creation of a category of empty freedom.

The main works using the motif of the f.m.c. were Cable's *The Grandissimes* (1880), Harris's "Free Joe and the Rest of the World" (1884), and Twain's *Huckleberry Finn* (1884). *The Grandissimes* was the first of these works to use the motif and was also the most obviously political. By giving signal prominence to the shadowy figure of Honoré Grandissime, f.m.c., Cable exposed the travesty of equality that blighted the lives of freedmen. Within four years of the

60

publication of Cable's novel, Harris and Twain each published works of their own in which the figure of an f.m.c. enabled them also to focus attention upon these victims of cruel delusion. It is not yet possible to ascribe a direct cause-and-effect relationship between *The Grandissimes* and these other works, although circumstantial evidence strongly suggests such a connection. But there can be no doubt that *The Grandissimes* broke literary trail in the South by its original use of realism and social criticism. At the very least, it supplied an example which Harris and Twain knew well, and it also demonstrated that there was a market for Southern literature which criticized Southern values. Most important, however, *The Grandissimes* headed a literary awakening to the deeper meanings of equality and freedom.

By virtue of their personal familiarity with free persons of color, Cable, Harris, and Twain had precise and practical knowledge of what these persons were and were not, in a legal as well as social sense. It is clear that members of the class were less than free. While the laws regarding free persons of color varied—sometimes substantially— from one Southern state to another, in general the laws were quite restrictive and backed up by much more repressive social mores. Louisiana, however, with whose laws Cable was obviously familiar, was one of the more liberal Southern states. As late as 1856, Judge Buchanan of the Louisiana Supreme Court could sum up what was a relatively mild and generous position:

> In the eye of the Louisiana law, there is, (with the exception of political rights, of certain social privileges, and of the obligation of jury and militia service) all the difference between a free man of color and a slave, that there is between a free man and a slave. The free man of color is capable of contracting. He can acquire by inheritance and transmit property by will. He is a competent witness in all civil suits. If he commits an offense against the laws, he is to be tried with the same formalities, and by the same tribunal, as the white man.[2]

The exceptions parenthetically referred to are spelled out more fully in the Black Code, based upon the 1724 Code Noir of French law which obtained until Louisiana joined the Union in 1804. The most important of them was the strict proscription of marriage between whites and coloreds, and the consequent illegitimacy of the children of such unions.[3] Originally, the Code Noir stipulated that these children would also become slaves "forever incapable of being set free," but at least one legal loophole was opened in 1791. In that year a law was passed in France declaring anyone free who set foot in France; a slave immediately became an ex-slave, and he would not revert to slave status again upon returning to French territory where slavery was legal. (This explains, in part, why Numa Grandissime sent his quadroon son Honoré to France.) Louisiana respected this law until 1846, when a law was passed nullifying (but not retroactively) freedom which derived from residence in a free area.[4]

Despite the law, however, as *The Grandissimes* shows, the social ostracism that attended free persons of color could be both oppressive and demeaning. In practice, the f.m.c. was usually dependent on the toleration of his community and was closely circumscribed in his activities. This can be seen by the steady conversion of social biases into increasingly constraining laws after Louisiana became a state. By 1806, for example, it became illegal for free persons of color to insult, strike, or even presume equality with whites; they were enjoined "to yield . . . in every occasion," and to always address whites respectfully.[5] (Just two years previous, Agricola Fusilier's imperious and insulting demands for this kind of deference from the f.m.c. had provoked their fatal conflict.) After 1807, numerous laws were passed "to prevent the emigration of free negroes and mulattoes into the Territory of Orleans," and to encourage emigration of free negroes from the state.[6] Such laws proliferated across the South in the decades preceding the Civil War.

Outside of Louisiana, the condition of f.m.c.'s was generally worse. In neighboring Mississippi, for example, f.m.c.'s could not even serve as witnesses against white men.[7] Georgia had harsh laws against them. Missouri, one of the border states, severely limited their social and economic activities:

> Particularly prominent were laws relating to the immigration of free Negroes; laws prohibiting meetings and associations with slaves without the consent of the owner; laws limiting the liquor trade among them [free Negroes], either by prohibiting the sale of liquor to them, or by prohibiting them from selling liquor; and finally laws creating such disabilities as to put them almost on a level with slaves in respect to the criminal law or other matters. . . . Free Negroes residing in Missouri had to procure a license to remain in the state, and in 1847 they were required to give a bond on going

from one county to another. In 1857, those going into a free State or territory, and returning, were subject to a fine of not less than $500, or imprisonment for one year, or both.[8]

The worst part of these laws was that they truly reflected Southern mores, and were not just the whims of a small ruling clique. The South was racist; its laws, like its mores, had never granted true equality or freedom to anyone who had any measurable quantity of Negro blood.

Cable had not begun as a Southern dissident. In his memoir, "My Politics," he recounts the process by which he came to repudiate the Southern strategy of undermining the Reconstruction and to condemn as "revolutionary disloyalty" the intention of white governments to return blacks to "arbitrary political subjugation."[9] Both his literary career and his political values were given their distinctive direction when his reading one day led him to the Black Code and he reacted to it "in sheer indignation."[10] *The Grandissimes* was Cable's resultant attack upon the virulent racism that was again resurgent across the South. By selecting a period, 1803–04, when that racism was in its incipient stage, Cable furnished himself with an appropriate historical analogy. By depicting the emptiness of the f.m.c.'s legal rights in that earlier period, Cable was able to use his analogy to focus upon the latter day process of reducing the new liberty of black freedmen to a hollow shell. Cable himself later summed up his opposition to the machinations of his own society with blunt succinctness: "Is the Freedman a free man? No."[11] Not to appreciate the force of this stand is to mistake Honoré Grandissime, f.m.c., for a sentimental figure. Thus Philip Butcher says of the f.m.c., "The quadroon, who explicitly refuses to be an advocate of any but his own personal and hopeless cause, symbolizes nothing but Cable's addiction to pathos."[12] Butcher sees both the dark Honoré and Palmyre primarily as quadroons; he therefore assumes that they represent an established literary tradition which based the pathos of their situation on their close resemblance to whites and not upon the evil of slavery.[13] But this view overlooks the issue that made *The Grandissimes* so famous a *cause celebre* in its day and continues to make the character of the dark Honoré so necessary an element of its social criticism. Cable, of course, condemned slavery root and branch, but it was dead as a legal institution and he did not waste his efforts upon a dead target. To him—and so the character functions in *The Grandissimes*—the f.m.c. symbolized the contemporary injustice to a class deprived of its legal rights by a majority whose prejudice was ignorant, lawless, and immoral. Had he created the f.m.c. as a stereotyped character who would conquer his own despair to become a dedicated advocate of hope, instead of an eminently human one whose personal sorrows overwhelmed him, Cable would have indeed been guilty of succumbing to sentimentalism. The final happiness of the principal whites in the novel—Joseph Frowenfeld, the white Honoré Grandissime, and Aurora and Clotilde Nancanou—*is* a romantic victory. They triumph over their temptations and environment and earn their rewards. But the end of the novel does not show a reform in the Creole society. Agricola Fusilier dies unreconstructed, refusing a priest, opposing the doctrine of equal rights, and with his last breath "haranguing" his family to "protect the race." The realistic conclusion of the novel is tragic, wrapped in the utter defeat of the f.m.c., and pessimistic, boding ill for the freedmen of the post-Reconstruction South.

Cable's historical analogy was not too subtle for the South; his pointed depiction of the f.m.c. was one of the first features of *The Grandissimes* to be criticized. According to Arlin Turner, Cable was accused in an otherwise favorable 1880 Southern review of having portrayed the f.m.c. in such a way as to pander to Northern wishes to see Southern intolerance denounced.[14] Later Southern critics became more antagonistic and came to read the novel as an indictment of the Old South culture which had condoned slavery and white supremacy before the Civil War and was unrepentant afterward. They were correct. By 1884, Cable's increasingly open and direct protests against the Southern handling of the "Negro Question" had made him unpopular in the South, including New Orleans, and prompted his move to the North. Cable's own view of the novel was unapologetic:

> I meant to make *The Grandissimes* as truly a political work as it has ever been called. . . . During all the time when the national majority was intensely interested in enforcing the principles and scheme of Reconstruction, my writings for Northern publication were unpolitical; and only just when the Reconstruction idea fell most hopelessly out of favor in the national mind I began to approve and advocate those principles; but always first in the South and then in the North. . . . My friends and kindred looked on with disapproval and dismay, and said all they could to restrain me.

"Why wantonly offend thousands of your 'own people'?" But I did not intend to offend. I wrote as near to truth and justice as I knew how. . . .[15]

From Cable's perspective, the truth should not have been offensive. What were offensive were the laws, legal and social, which openly chained, maimed, and killed the magnificent Bras-Coupé; which just as surely, though more insidiously, destroyed the fine and sensitive Honoré Grandissime, f.m.c.; and which were now re-subjugating the freedmen.

There were so few good Southern writers at the time of the publication of *The Grandissimes* that they were alert to each other's work. The stories that Cable had written in the 1870s for *Scribner's* and *Appleton's Journal* and had collected and published in 1879 as *Old Creole Days* had attracted much favorable attention to him in the South as well as in the rest of the country. One of the most discerning and appreciative of Cable's Southern readers was Joel Chandler Harris. A journalist with the Atlanta *Constitution* since 1876, Harris quickly began attracting commendation for both his editorials and the dialect sketches which developed into the renowned Uncle Remus stories. Harris had an avid and informed interest in developing mature literature in the South. In an 1879 article, Harris sharply scored the drivel which passed as literature in the South merely because it reflected "sectionalism." "The stuff we are in the habit of calling Southern literature is not only a burlesque upon literary art, but a humiliation and a disgrace to the people whose culture it is supposed to represent."[16]

That Harris approved of Cable and specifically appreciated *The Grandissimes* is evident from an editorial he wrote in 1881, by which time *The Grandissimes* was already being attacked—sometimes viciously—across the South. Julia Collier Harris describes Harris's editorial as deploring "the risk of ostracism confronting the Southern writer when adhering to strictly impartial or frankly realistic delineation of character and customs."[17] After citing a particularly scurrilous pamphlet that had moved him to defend Cable, Harris wrote that "if the South is ever to make any permanent or important contribution to the literature of the world, we must get over our self-consciousness

and so control our sensitiveness as to be able to regard with indif-
ference—nay, with complacence—the impulse of criticism which
prompts and spurs every literary man and woman whose work is
genuine. We must not forget that real literary art is absolutely impartial and invariably just. None other can endure."[18] Under the circumstances, at the very least this editorial must be deemed courageous.
But there is also an element of fellow feeling in it, the understanding
sympathy one like mind has for another.

The kindred spirits met the next year in New Orleans. Mark Twain
arranged the meeting (later immortalized in Chapter 47 of *Life on the
Mississippi*) between himself, Cable, and Harris. Exactly what they
discussed in private is not a matter of record, but it would have been
astonishing if they had not discussed their craft, the South, and the
"Negro Question." Cable had been the first of the three to apply
realism to the depiction of Southern characters and customs. Twain in
1882 was already on the way with *Huckleberry Finn* in progress.
Harris, as his editorials indicate, was on the brink. *The Grandissimes*
had stirred him deeply. But what was there to stir?

Harris's deeper seriousness has increasingly attracted and occupied
scholarly interest. Howard W. Odum characterized his work as that of
a "vigorous realist, in which he never forgot the tragedies of the South,
the poor white man, the darker aspects of slavery, the separation of
families, and the hypocricies [sic] reflected in sentimentality and
religiosity."[19] R. Bruce Bickley, Jr. quotes Harris as saying in 1877 that
"even the bare suggestion of [slavery's] reëstablishment is unsavory,"
and observes that though "Harris shared in the racial prejudices of his
day, he affirmed the integrity of all individuals, whether black or
white; and he could not countenance unjust or inhumane actions by
any member of the human race."[20] It is not yet fully resolved just how
liberal or conservative Harris was, but it is significant that one of his
strongest criticisms of Old South values is centered around an f.m.c. in
the story "Free Joe and the Rest of the World."

Generally conceded to be "one of the most memorable of all Harris's non-folklore stories of the old South,"[21] "Free Joe" has both depth
and power. Hubbell calls it Harris's most striking treatment of the
Negro outside of the Uncle Remus stories, and perceptively observes
that "this tragic story of a free Negro in slavery times . . . could hardly

have been written by any other Southern writer of the nineteenth century except perhaps George W. Cable."[22] As with many of his other tales, folklore as well as non-folklore, this story can be read as either sentimentalism or realism, though the deeper values are more abundant on the realistic side. Harris demonstrates in it a vivid awareness of the harsh Georgia laws and practices in regard to free persons of color. It was based, in fact, upon a personal recollection from his own boyhood.[23] The story hinges upon a central irony concerning Free Joe's "peculiar condition": "that though he was free he was more helpless than any slave."[24] Any white man could order him around; he had no defender. He felt obliged to stay apart from slaves, and they shunned him. He had no hope of winning kindness and appreciation, only toleration. When his wife was sold to a distant buyer by a spiteful master—free Negroes had no legal rights to wives or children who were slaves—he was left alone except for his dog. When the dog was killed by the hounds of the spiteful master, Free Joe was left desolate, without a friend in the world. He was found dead one morning, sitting against a tree, facing towards the plantation where his wife used to work. "His clothes were ragged; his hands were rough and callous; his shoes were literally tied together with strings; he was shabby in the extreme. A passer-by, glancing at him, could have no idea that such a humble creature had been summoned as a witness before the Lord God of Hosts."[25]

Harris, like Cable, was a devout man. The story's last line alludes to a higher judge than any on earth, and one who holds all men equal before Him, without reference to color or status. "Free Joe" despite its gentleness is, in the final analysis, a judgmental story. It is also a pessimistic story. In it, though he did not share Cable's reforming zeal, Harris also contemplated the future of the black freedman in the new South, and Free Joe fared no better than had Honoré Grandissime, f.m.c.

Beyond what might be inferred from the text of the story, there is also external evidence that suggests that "Free Joe" might have been an expression of sympathy for black freedmen. Indeed, the story's publication in the midst of a magazine controversy between his friends over the status of blacks in the New South seems too timely to have been entirely coincidental. In November 1884, three years after he defended *The Grandissimes* and two years after he met Cable and Twain, Harris published the story in the *Century* "with the encouragement and editorial assistance of Richard Watson Gilder,"[26] the editor and also a personal friend of Cable and Twain. In the December number of the *Century* appeared the first of three installments of *Huckleberry Finn* (the other two appeared in January and February 1885). In January appeared Cable's stinging indictment of the South, "The Freedman's Case in Equity," and in April a rebuttal, "In Plain Black and White," by Henry W. Grady.[27] Grady was one of two associate editors of the Atlanta *Constitution*; the other one was Harris. Grady was an exponent of the New South and an especial advocate of its industrialization. According to Paul M. Cousins, Harris remained wary of this development and preferred to channel his efforts towards promoting "a Southern literary renaissance and healing the sectional wounds left by the Civil War and the Reconstruction."[28] Although Harris and Grady were friends as well as close colleagues, it is obvious that there were important areas about which they were not in substantial agreement. Cousins has listed one. Literary and social judgments must have been others.

Addressing himself to "The Freedman's Case," Grady says, "In this article, as in his works, the singular tenderness and beauty of which have justly made him famous, Mr. Cable is sentimental rather than practical."[29] A contrast of this remark with Harris's 1881 defense of *The Grandissimes* clearly reveals the distance between the two men's estimates of Cable's writing. Grady advocated the "separate but equal" position. The separation part is clear enough, but he had difficulties with the explanation of equality. As Grady saw it, though the abolition of slavery was a good consequence of the war, the wisdom of allowing blacks to vote was doubtful, and the insistence that blacks should have the same social and civil rights was "wrongheaded." Confident that the whites of his time, and for many generations to come, would continue to dominate such qualities as "intelligence, character, and property," and would treat blacks fairly and wisely, Grady concluded his discussion with these words from the mouth of the personified South: "Leave this problem to my working out. I will solve it in calmness and deliberation, without passion or prejudice, and with full regard for the unspeakable equities it holds.

Judge me rigidly, but judge me by my works!"[30] It was a beautiful theory, but it is difficult to reconcile with Harris's story and with the reality of Southern society at the time. "Free Joe" is not just about an f.m.c.; it is also about a typical Southern town, "the rest of the world." If Grady had read the story, he showed no signs of having understood it. Harris, on the other hand, surely knew Grady's position but evidently was not convinced by it. Harris's use of the f.m.c., therefore, illuminates not only his sympathy for blacks, but for the black freedmen whose rights were at issue.

The relationship between Cable and Mark Twain began in the summer of 1881 when Cable, riding high on the swell of popularity that followed the publication of *The Grandissimes*, visited Hartford, Connecticut, and was introduced to Twain. The relationship grew the following summer, when Twain arranged the meeting in New Orleans, and probably reached its peak during the famous four-month lecture tour that Twain organized for himself and Cable from November 1884 to February 1885.

Undoubtedly Cable influenced Twain, although the specifics are admittedly speculative. But an important clue is evident in *Life on the Mississippi*, in which Twain describes Cable as "the South's finest literary genius, the author of *The Grandissimes*. In him the South has found a masterly delineator of its interior life and its history."[31] Inasmuch as *Huckleberry Finn* was completed in 1883 and published in 1884, it is most likely that whatever influence Cable had upon Twain would show up in that novel, itself a "masterly delineation" of the South's "interior life and its history." Guy Cardwell conjectures that Cable's influence on *Huckleberry Finn* was strong in 1881–1883 and probably most important "with respect to its social and poetic attitudes at points where Twain explores the nature of culture and the nature of men's relationships within a culture."[32] Certainly, in a general sense, the earlier novel both pioneered a realistic analysis of the South and also encouraged Twain to make his own ventures in this vein. But also in its depiction of the f.m.c., *The Grandissimes* may well have opened Twain's eyes to the literary possibilities inherent in the figure, for he used it significantly in *Huckleberry Finn*.

Twain's use of the f.m.c. surfaces in Chapter 42, when Tom Sawyer ends the sequence of romantic antics at the end of the novel by dramatically announcing Jim's freedom: "Turn him loose! he ain't no slave; he's as free as any other cretur that walks this earth!"[33] All along, Tom had known that Miss Watson had manumitted Jim. It is an ending that has surprised and disappointed many critics, especially in recent times. But the ending is ironic rather than simple, and need not be considered disappointing. Twain knew how far Jim as an f.m.c. would be from the reality of freedom. If Jim returned to St. Petersburg, the laws of Missouri would have prevented him not only from being free in the political sense that he would be equal to whites, but also in the social and economic senses as well. Though Jim, in a manner of speaking, was his own property as an f.m.c. ("I owns myself, en I's wuth eight hund'd dollars"), he would not own his wife and two children, who were still slaves. Practically speaking, as far as his family was concerned, the same two options would have been available to Jim as either an escaped slave or an f.m.c. As Jim knew, he could either work to free his wife and then save their combined wages to buy his children, if their master would sell them; or he could hire an abolitionist to steal them. In short, Jim's freedom came down to "his right to return to St. Petersburg and work like a slave to earn at a pitiful wage the staggering sum he needed to buy his wife and children."[34] Jim's freedom is only illusory, and by deliberately having Tom proclaim that "he's as free as any cretur that walks this earth!" Twain did not write a novel that fails to promote a conception of freedom, but rather a novel which powerfully, poignantly, and successfully *denies* freedom.[35] Where Cable and Harris restricted their uses of the f.m.c. to signify pessimistically the black freedman of the post-Civil War South, Twain used the f.m.c. more broadly to signify pessimistically all men. In *Huckleberry Finn* all men are represented, ironically, as laboring under the same cruel delusion of mock freedom as the free persons of color.

No other work by Twain makes such pointed use of an f.m.c., but the influence of the f.m.c. persists in two additional works of the 1880s. One of them is "Huck Finn and Tom Sawyer among the Indians," the unfinished sequel to *Huckleberry Finn*. In it, Jim joins Huck and Tom on their trip into the Territory because "there was white men around our little town that was plenty mean enough and ornery enough to steal Jim's papers from him and sell him down the river again."[36] This quote alone would amply document Twain's sensitivity to the precariousness of an f.m.c.'s freedom. The influence of the f.m.c. appears even more powerfully in *Connecticut Yankee* (1889). In this book, set in sixth century A.D. England, the place of the f.m.c. is filled, of course, by white "freemen." Hank Morgan's commentary on them points up their essential similarities to the f.m.c.'s of nineteenth century America. "And yet they were not slaves, not chattels. By a sarcasm of law and phrase they were freemen."[37] They were "free" only in comparison to actual slaves; to all other classes they were humble, obedient, and self-deprecating. They were like the f.m.c.'s of Twain's Missouri boyhood, or of post-1806 Louisiana—or the freedmen of the post-Reconstruction South.

In this perforce brief and limited comparison of Cable, Harris, and Twain, two salient topics have been explored: *The Grandissimes'* original use of the f.m.c. motif, and the powerful uses to which it was put by all three authors in their literature of the 1880s. Again, it is not necessary to claim that but for *The Grandissimes*, Harris and Twain might not have used f.m.c.'s in their own works. But it would be an unusually puristic position which would deny any weight to the circumstantial evidence of its importance to the other two authors: its publication four years before their own literary use of the f.m.c., the fact that Harris and Twain both read the novel when it first came out, and the fact that Cable was in friendly contact with Twain from 1881 and Harris from 1882. Further, *The Grandissimes* was the opening gun in the literary protest, in which all three authors joined, against the post-Reconstruction move in the South to abridge the rights of black freedmen.

The works that have been discussed are all too rich and complex to imply that a single theme, or motif, or effect can adequately sum up their significance, or even their relationship to each other. It has not been my purpose to so reduce them. Rather, I have attempted to trace out some likely inferences of a single shared—and important—motif. At precisely the moment the South regressed in its adherence to the principles of equality and freedom, its three leading authors affirmed their own concern for them. That Cable, Harris, and Twain were Southerners, born and bred, gave their voices an authenticity and authority that no others could supply. In their own time, they were in the minority, but in the fullness of time they have prevailed.

NOTES

[1]Other references to Cable's use of a historical parallel (though not to the part the f.m.c. played in it) include Arlin Turner, "Introduction," *Creoles and Cajuns* (Garden City, N.Y.: Doubleday, 1959), p. 12; and R.N. Mehta, "Cable's Handling of the Political Theme in *The Grandissimes,*" *Indian Studies in American Fiction,* eds. M.K. Naik, S.K. Desai, and S. Mokashi-Punekar (Dharwar, India: Macmillan, 1974), p. 97.

[2]Helen Tunnicliff Catteral, ed., *Judicial Cases Concerning American Slavery and the Negro,* III (Washington, D.C.: G.P.O., 1932), p. 393.

[3]Charles Gayarré, *History of Louisiana,* I (New York: Widdleton, 1886), article 6, pp. 531–32. Gayarré's *History* was an important source for Cable.

[4]Catteral, III, p. 389.

[5]"Article 40," *Digest of the Laws Relative to Slaves and Free People of Colour in the State of Louisiana* (New Orleans: Louisiana Constitutional and Anti-Fanatical Society, 1835), p. 8. H.E. Sterkx's book, *The Free Negro in Ante-Bellum Louisiana* (Rutherford, N.J.: Fairleigh Dickinson Univ. Press, 1972), is a valuable study which documents with additional detail the progressive deterioration of f.m.c. status in Louisiana.

[6]*Digest, passim,* pp. 14–21. See also Sterkx, pp. 91–117.

[7]William R. Hogan and Edwin A. Davis, "Introduction," *William Johnson's Natchez* (Baton Rouge: Louisiana State Univ. Press, 1951), p. 55. This book, the edited diary of a free man of color, is an excellent account of what it meant to be an f.m.c. in Mississippi. Hamilton Basso's *The Light Infantry Ball* (Garden City: Doubleday, 1959) deals fictionally with the same subject.

[8]Henry W. Farnam, *Chapters in the History of Social Legislation in the United States to 1860,* ed. Clive Day (Washington, D.C.: G.P.O., 1938), pp. 200, 202.

[9]"My Politics," *The Negro Question,* ed. Arlin Turner (New York: Norton, 1958), pp. 7–8.

[10]"My Politics," p. 11.

[11]"The Freedman's Case in Equity," *The Negro Question,* p. 73.

[12]Philip Butcher, *George Washington Cable* (New York: Twayne, 1962), p. 50.

[13]Butcher, p. 51.

[14]Arlin Turner, *George W. Cable: A Biography* (Baton Rouge: Louisiana State Univ. Press, 1966), p. 101. The initial reception of the novel, according to Turner (p. 100), was highly favorable. It was immediately recognized as a major literary event and praised in such national magazines as *Scribner's,* the *Atlantic,* the *Nation,* and *Appleton's Journal.* See also "Southern Literature," *Scribner's,* 22 (May-October 1881), 785–786. The one major exception to this initial acclaim was some resentment expressed by the Creole press. Opposition soon developed in other Southern quarters, however.

[15]"My Politics," p. 14.

[16]Quoted in R. Bruce Bickley, Jr., *Joel Chandler Harris* (Boston: Twayne, 1978), p. 35.

[17]Julia Collier Harris, *Joel Chandler Harris: Editor and Essayist* (Chapel Hill: Univ. of North Carolina Press, 1931), p. 46.

[18]Quoted in Julia Collier Harris, pp. 46–47.

[19]Quoted in Paul M. Cousins, *Joel Chandler Harris* (Baton Rouge: Louisiana State Univ. Press, 1968), pp. 222–23.

[20]Bickley, p. 36.

[21]Cousins, p. 146, and Bickley, p. 114.

[22]Jay Hubbell, *The South in American Literature: 1607–1900* (Durham: Duke Univ. Press, 1954), p. 791.

[23]*On the Plantation* (New York: Appleton, 1892), pp. 230–31.

[24]"Free Joe and the Rest of the World," *Free Joe and Other Georgian Sketches* (New York: P.F. Collier, 1887), p. 12.

[25]"Free Joe," p. 29.

[26]Bickley, p. 48.

[27]Henry W. Grady, "In Plain Black and White: A Reply to Mr. Cable," *Century*, 29, 909–17. Some possible evidence of editorial favoritism might be inferred from the placing of Cable's autobiographical piece, "New Orleans Before the Capture," immediately after Grady's article. Grady had implied that Cable was not a true Southerner; Cable's piece is a vivid recollection, from a Southern point of view, of New Orleans' last days as a Confederate city.

[28]Cousins, p. 94.

[29]Grady, p. 909.

[30]Grady, p. 917.

[31]Mark Twain, *Life on the Mississippi*, intro. Dixon Wecter (New York: Harper and Bros., 1950), p. 355. See also Chapters 46 and 47.

[32]Guy A. Cardwell, *Twins of Genius* (London: Neville Spearman, 1962), pp. 70–71.

[33]*Huckleberry Finn*, ed. Henry Nash Smith (Boston: Houghton, Mifflin, 1958), p. 241.

[34]Lawrence I. Berkove, "The 'Poor Players' of *Huckleberry Finn*," *Papers of the Michigan Academy of Science, Arts, and Letters*, 52 (1968), p. 308.

[35]In my article, which affirms both structural and thematic unity in *Huckleberry Finn*, I develop this interpretation in much greater detail.

[36]Mark Twain, "Huck Finn and Tom Sawyer among the Indians," *Mark Twain's Hannibal, Huck and Tom*, ed. Walter Blair (Berkeley: University of California, 1969), p. 93. The fragment was probably written in 1884. An additional reference to the precarious freedom of f.m.c.'s occurs in *Connecticut Yankee*. After Hank Morgan and King Arthur were sold as slaves at an auction because the law required them to prove that they were not slaves, and they could not, Hank reflects: "This same infernal law had existed in our own South in my own time, more than thirteen hundred years later, and under it hundreds of freemen who could not prove that they were freemen were sold into life-long slavery without the circumstance making any particular impression upon me; but the minute law and the auction block came into my personal experience, a thing which had been merely improper before became suddenly hellish. Well, that's the way we are made." *A Connecticut Yankee in King Arthur's Court* (San Francisco: Chandler, 1963), p. 449.

[37]*Connecticut Yankee*, p. 154.

Lions Rampant:
Agricola Fusilier and Bras-Coupé as Antithetical Doubles in The Grandissimes

JOSEPH J. EGAN

Among the most abiding devices in fiction is the employment of characters with opposing personalities as doubles to achieve symbolic truth. Indeed, this device, often centering on pairs of near relatives, pervades the literature of the last century—the century in which George Washington Cable wrote *The Grandissimes*—as witness such diverse works as Eliot's *Middlemarch*, Dostoyevsky's *The Brothers Karamazov*, Twain's *Pudd'nhead Wilson*, and Stevenson's *The Master of Ballantrae*. More than twenty years ago, Newton Arvin recognized this kinsman-alter ego motif in *The Grandissimes* itself:

> The three forms that human antagonism takes in the novel—familial, political, racial—are all seen as involving a confusion of emotions, attraction as well as repulsion, closeness as well as division, love as well as hatred. The central token of this is the relation between the "two Honorés" (their names are identical)—the white Honoré, the Creole gentleman, and the quadroon Honoré, his declassed and alienated half-brother. There is a curious anticipation, in this pairing, of the intense and almost amorous relation between Henry Sutpen and his mulatto half-brother, Charles Bon, in Faulkner's *Absalom, Absalom!* as there is an anticipation in the essentially sisterly relation between Aurore Nancanou and the quadroon Palmyre of the essentially brotherly relation between Bayard Sartoris and Ringo in *The Unvanquished*. Like Faulkner, Cable had an intuition of the inescapable and profound dependence upon each other—a dependence like that of inimical brothers—of the two races.[1]

There is in *The Grandissimes* perhaps another, highly ironic, pairing of doubles, brothers now in the larger sense that all men are brothers: Agricola Fusilier and Bras-Coupé.

On the surface, of course, these two men seem to have little in

74

common. Agricola, patriarch of the Grandissime-Fusilier family, speaks for Creole privilege and white supremacy; Bras-Coupé, the outlawed slave, dares to challenge all the assumptions of which Agricola is the representative. A closer study of the two, however, reveals striking similarities, which in their symbolic reverberations encompass the mythic truth of Cable's novel. Significantly, when Bras-Coupé leaves the incongruously named slave ship, "the good schooner *Egalité*" (p. 169) and sets foot on Louisiana soil, the first person he encounters is Agricola Fusilier: "When Bras-Coupé staggered ashore, he stood but a moment among a drove of 'likely boys,' before Agricola Fusilier, managing the business adventures of the Grandissime estate, as well as the residents thereon, and struck with admiration for the physical beauties of the chieftain (a man may even fancy a negro—as a negro), bought the lot, and loth to resell him with the rest to some unappreciative 'Cadian, induced Don José Martinez' overseer to become his purchaser" (p. 170). The admiration Agricola at this point feels for Bras-Coupé suggests that the two men, opposites though they are, share common characteristics—and, finally, a common fate.

In physical appearance and manner—except for obvious differences of race and age—Agricola and Bras-Coupé are remarkably alike. Early in the book Cable supplies us with a detailed description of the old Creole: "The person who confronted the apothecary was a large, heavily built, but well molded and vigorous man, of whom one might say that he was adorned with old age. His brow was dark, and furrowed partly by time and partly by a persistent ostentatious frown. His eyes were large, black, and bold, and the gray locks above them curled short and harsh like the front of a bull. His nose was fine and strong" (p. 47). Later, Doctor Keene observes that Agricola is as strong "as an orang-outang" (p. 101). Bras-Coupé, the black giant, is "an athlete of superb figure" (p. 190), with a "fine, straight nose" (p. 172) and a countenance capable of "a fixed frown" (p. 192); in his strength and awesome presence he is likened to a "rhinoceros" (p. 172) and the "African buffalo" (p. 173).

In his description of both men, Cable gives a special emphasis to animal imagery. Perhaps the animal most frequently used as a metaphor in delineating the physical—and psychological—qualities of this antithetical pair is the lion. Throughout the novel, particularly in Chapter 15, entitled "Rolled in the Dust," Agricola is called "the lion"—"a voice that, once heard, was always known,—deep and pompous, as if a lion roared" (p. 83). In like manner, the lion image becomes associated with Bras-Coupé: "Bras-Coupé . . . laid his paw upon his fellow-bridegroom's shoulder" (p. 180). . . . "With an easy motion, but quick as lightning, as a lion sets foot on a dog, he caught her by the arm" (p. 187). In addition to its power and magnificence, Cable makes use of the lion's regal connotations to complete his portraits of Agricola and Bras-Coupé and to suggest further the resemblance between the two. As patriarch of the Grandissime-Fusilier dynasty, Agricola fancies himself an aristocrat among aristocrats—the "pure white" (p. 59) Louisiana Creoles: "H-my young friend . . . when I, Agricola Fusilier, pronounce you a professor, you are a professor. Louisiana will not look to *you* for your credentials; she will look to me!" (p. 53). At the beginning of Chapter 28, "The Story of Bras-Coupé," we learn that the mighty Jaloff had been "a prince among his people" (p. 169) and possesses a "herculean puissance which formerly in Africa had made him the terror of the battle" (p. 171).

The aristocratic pretensions of Agricola and Bras-Coupé (the Creole wears "his dress-sword" [p. 181] and the African bedecks himself with "red and blue regimentals" [p. 178] the night of the fateful double wedding) prompt them to denigrate their fellowmen—especially, defenseless blacks—and to disdain all physical labor. Observes Agricola: "Not that there is a prejudice against the negro. By no means. Wherever he can be of any service in a strictly menial capacity we kindly and generously tolerate his presence" (p. 59). Such opinions the Creole carries to his grave: "Society has pyramids to build which make menials a necessity, and Nature furnishes the menials all in dark uniform" (p. 327). Bras-Coupé's attitude towards work and servitude, formed by "African international law" (p. 174), is not far different from Agricola's own:

> When one day he had come to be quite himself, he was invited out into the sunshine, and escorted by the driver (a sort of foreman to the overseer), went forth dimly wondering. They reached a field where some men and women were hoeing. He had seen men and women—subjects of his—labor—a little—in Africa. The driver handed him a hoe; he examined it with silent interest—until by signs he was requested to join the pastime.

"What?"

He spoke, not with his lips, but with the recoil of his splendid frame and the ferocious expansion of his eyes. This invitation was a cataract of lightning leaping down an ink-black sky. In one instant of all-pervading clearness he read his sentence—WORK.

Bras-Coupé was six feet five. With a sweep as quick as instinct the back of the hoe smote the driver full in the head. Next, the prince lifted the nearest Congo crosswise, brought thirty-two teeth together in his wildly kicking leg and cast him away as a bad morsel. (pp. 171–72)

Ironically, owing to their sense of personal superiority, these almost intransigent rivals view each other with consummate scorn: whereas Bras-Coupé calls Agricola "a contemptible *dotchian* (white trash)" (p. 178), the old man, long after the African's mutilation and tragic death, complains of being "taunted with the righteous hamstringing of a dangerous runaway" (p. 317). One should note that when Bras-Coupé is driven to seek refuge in the infernal swamp after striking Don José, his Spanish-Creole master, his predicament becomes a species of paying the piper: "Many a wretch in his native wilderness has Bras-Coupé himself, in palmier days, driven to just such an existence, to escape the chains and horrors of the barracoons; therefore not a whit broods he over man's inhumanity, but, taking the affair as a matter of course, casts about him for a future" (p. 182).

The noble and priestly castes are closely related in societies recognizing strict hierarchic divisions; hence it is appropriate that Agricola, the majestic Creole, and Bras-Coupé, the African prince, should both espouse their own stylized "religions," although even in death neither has any use for the services of a representative of orthodoxy—a Roman Catholic priest. Agricola, "the aged high-priest of a doomed civilization" (p. 324), wears "a beard that swept down over his broad breast like the beard of a prophet" (p. 47), while Bras-Coupé is a voudou, who "hears the voice of zombis" (p. 179) and "call[s] Voudou-Magnan" (p. 179) to curse the land of his white master.

The deaths of Bras-Coupé and old Fusilier parallel each other in several ways. Near death, Bras-Coupé revokes the supposed spell he has cast on Don José, who in dying has begged the African's forgiveness, and responds with generous sympathies to his master's widow and her baby:

The lady came, her infant boy in her arms, knelt down beside the bed of sweet grass and set the child within the hollow of the African's arm. Bras-Coupé turned his gaze upon it; it smiled, its mother's smile, and put its hand upon the runaway's face, and the first tears of Bras-Coupé's life, the dying testimony of his humanity, gushed from his eyes and rolled down his cheek upon the infant's hand. He laid his own tenderly upon the babe's forehead, then removing it, waved it abroad, inaudibly moved his lips, dropped his arm, and closed his eyes. The curse was lifted. (p. 193)

At the very moment of his death, Bras-Coupé expresses the joyous conviction that he is going "To—Africa" (p. 193). Agricola, too, "lifts a curse"—one that has perpetuated the feud between the Grandissimes and the De Grapions—when he summons the white Honoré and Aurore Nancanou to his deathbed and, clasping the hands of each, rectifies a wrong of two decades' standing: "Aurore De Gra—I pledge'—pledge'—pledged—this union—to your fa—father—twen-ty—years—ago" (p. 328). Like Bras-Coupé, Agricola dies with the name of his home upon his lips: "Louis—Louisian—a—for—ever!" (p. 328).

The dying attempts of Bras-Coupé and Agricola Fusilier to make amends for past hatred help to sustain the novel's vision of hope. In fact, the embrace of Honoré and Aurore, with which *The Grandissimes* ends, intimates the belief that human hostilities—familial, racial, and national—can one day be resolved. But the hope Cable expresses is modulated. Since Bras-Coupé and Fusilier represent outmoded or attenuated forms of aristocracy, total reconciliation can occur only in succeeding generations and therefore lies beyond the compass of the novel. Bras-Coupé's final thoughts had been about Africa; similarly, as he dies, Agricola exhorts his kinsmen to "protect the race!" (p. 328) of white "Louisiana forever" from the encroach-ment of *Américain* political and social reform, an exhortation that is carved on his tomb. Cable's narrator immediately remarks the in-adequacy of such narrow affiliations: "And yet the family committee that ordered the inscription, the mason who cut it in the marble—himself a sort of half-Grandissime, half-nobody—and even the fair women who each eve of All Saints came, attended by flower-laden slave girls, to lay coronals upon the old man's tomb, felt, feebly at first, and more and more distinctly as years went by, that Forever was a trifle long for one to confine one's patriotic affection to a small fraction of a great country" (p. 329).

The spiritual and psychological ruin that racial antagonism and exploitation bring to the life of man is reflected in the obscene mutilation and hamstringing of Bras-Coupé and, of course, in his metaphorical name. As Cable's narrator explains, Bras-Coupé (the name in French means "the Arm Cut Off") "made himself a type of all Slavery, turning into flesh and blood the truth that all Slavery is maiming" (p. 171). Yet slavery maims the perpetrator with the victim. Despite his strength and vigor, Agricola is an *old* man, who at moments seems oddly feeble: "There were times when it took but little to make Agricola stumble" (p. 53). Like Bras-Coupé's, his name also carries symbolic overtones: *Agricola* is the Latin word for farmer, and *Fusilier* in French indicates a soldier armed with a musket. Agricola becomes the figure of the agrarian interests of Southern patrician society, which would later take up arms in a civil war to defend its obsolete prerogatives and would, as a consequence, experience a "maiming" defeat.

Racial hostility, then, destroys not only the black man but also the white. In his violent attack on the black Honoré Grandissime, "free man of color," Agricola is fatally stabbed, falling victim to his own terrible prejudice. The black Honoré is central to the racial clash in *The Grandissimes*, for both races contend within him. As the elder son of Numa Grandissime, the dark Honoré is the rightful heir of the Grandissime-Fusilier dynasty, but because of his mother's blood, the family competency passes from him to his younger half-brother, the white Honoré. Honoré Grandissime, f.m.c., has other ties with the black race and thus also with Agricola, its principal adversary. His love for the exquisite quadroon Palmyre links Honoré to Bras-Coupé, her husband. Accordingly, Agricola incurs the dual wrath of Honoré and Palmyre: he foils Honoré's attempt to marry Palmyre, just as he had foiled her desire to employ Bras-Coupé's "mighty arm" (p. 178) as a weapon of insurrection against himself and the intolerance he represents. Yet, even after her husband's death, Palmyre continues to use his talismanic power in the hope that her voudou enchantments will have that much more effect on Agricola; her most potent grigri is a small black coffin containing "the image, in myrtle-wax, moulded and painted with some rude skill, of a negro's bloody arm cut off near the shoulder—a *bras-coupé*—with a dirk grasped in its hand" (p. 314). In the end, however, it is, as we have seen, the black Honoré and especially the old Creole's own irrational animosity, not Bras-Coupé or voudou, that bring Agricola down.

Although Aurore and the white Honoré mend old family wounds, both Palmyre and the f.m.c. are defeated—she by living a life of lonely exile in Bordeaux, a life that symbolically parallels Bras-Coupé's retreat to the swamp; he through "suicide," the inevitable result of social injustice: "My-de-seh . . . you speak like a true Anglo-Saxon; but, sir! how many, many communities have *committed suicide*. And this one?—why, it is *just* the kind to do it!" (p. 94). The defeat of these two characters derives from the insensate racial antagonism pervading life in Cable's novel; at the symbolic heart of it all are the antithetical, yet wryly similar, figures of Agricola Fusilier and Bras-Coupé. These fierce doubles, these warring lions, each the victim of virulent prejudice, give emphatic testimony to the manifold destruction—and self-destruction—accompanying malice and intolerance. There are universal overtones here, mythic suggestions that lift the meaning of the novel beyond the fate of Agricola Fusilier and Bras-Coupé, beyond Louisiana herself, beyond time and place, to the spirit of man:

> One great general subject of thought now is human rights,—universal human rights. The entire literature of the world is becoming tinctured with contradictions of the dogmas upon which society in this section is built. Human rights is, of all subjects, the one upon which this community is most violently determined to hear no discussion. It has pronounced that slavery and caste are right, and sealed up the whole subject. What, then, will they do with the world's literature? They will coldly decline to look at it, and will become, more and more as the world moves on, a comparatively illiterate people. (p. 143)

By skillful juxtaposition of Agricola Fusilier and Bras-Coupé, Cable's *The Grandissimes* eloquently, though sadly, describes the profound human tragedy attendant upon the refusal to recognize the brotherhood of all men.

NOTE

[1]Newton Arvin, Introduction, *The Grandissimes* by George W. Cable (New York: Hill and Wang, 1957), p. x. Citations to Cable's novel will be to this edition. (*The Grandissimes* anticipates Faulkner's work—*The Bear* most obviously—in other ways: "Family Trees," Chapter 4 of Cable's novel, incorporates the kind of elaborate genealogical charting so closely associated with Faulkner's canon.)

The Grandissimes:
An Annotated Bibliography (1880–1979)

ANTHONY J. ADAM AND SARA McCASLIN

This bibliography of criticism of *The Grandissimes* includes books, essays, and contemporary reviews which treat the novel and excludes dissertations, theses, and criticism in foreign languages. To simplify annotations, we have abbreviated *The Grandissimes* to *G*. All citations from Turner, *Critical Essays* refer to Arlin Turner's *Critical Essays on George Washington Cable* (Boston: G.K. Hall, 1980). The bibliography includes material from 1880–1979, with the addition of the essays appearing in this present collection.

Aaron, Daniel. "George Washington Cable." Rpt. from *The Unwritten War: American Writers and the Civil War* (New York: Alfred A. Knopf, 1973), pp. 272–82. Rpt. in Turner, *Critical Essays*, pp. 229–39.

A brief overview of the novel which includes a number of important insights relative to a better understanding of Cable's writing. Aaron points out that Cable is not unlike his hero, Frowenfeld, an outsider who is sickened by the treatment of blacks under the code of the times and appalled at the consequences of miscegenation. Aaron also compares *G* to *Uncle Tom's Cabin*, which Cable claimed to have read at age nine. Cable's blacks are distinguished from Stowe's "cartoons" by the variety and subtlety of portraiture.

Arvin, Newton. "Introduction," to Cable's *The Grandissimes*. American Century Series (New York: Sagamore Press, 1957), pp. v–xi. Rpt. in Turner, *Critical Essays*, pp. 180–84.

The problem of *G* arises from Cable's duality of mind. On the one hand, he had a strong sentimental streak which gave a false note even to the story of Bras-Coupé. Yet he also had a sharp eye for ordinary social reality, coupled with a strongly developed critical sense and a love for documented fact. The scenes in *G* may be romantic, but they have a strong realistic tone. Cable also had a strong feeling for the violent nature which seems so much a part of Southern life.

Barrie, James M. "A Note on Mr. Cable's *The Grandissimes.*" *Bookman*, 7 (July 1898), pp. 401–3. Rpt. in Turner, *Critical Essays*, pp. 112–14. This "note" is essentially the same as the "note" to *The Grandissimes* (London: Hodder and Stoughton, 1898), pp. xi–xv, and "Two Prefaces by Mr. Barrie" in *Academy*, 53 (June 4, 1891), p. 604.

General impressionistic study of *G*. Barrie notes that one may still see the homes of Aurora in the Quarter, where was played "one of the prettiest love scenes in any language." If Aurora had been from a later age, she might not have approved of Cable. Gradually one realizes that the French-English struggles in New Orleans are just trumpery, and that even the blacks would wait their turn so that the Creoles could finally get the justice due them.

Baskerville, W. M. "George W. Cable." *Chautauquan*, 25 (May 1897), pp. 179–84. Rpt. in Turner, *Critical Essays*, pp. 106–11.

In *G* Cable forsook the paths of character study and returned to the old romance. Yet he is modern and has taken with him the eye for the picturesque, the artist's fine sense of workmanship, and the artist's aim of producing effect in a natural way. Cable seems to have approached his subject from the point of view of Rousseau and the French Revolution. But too frequently the author appears on the scene above his characters. At such times he makes sententious comments or utters commonplaces universally accepted, and from this point of view the novel is blemished. Partisan feeling dulls Cable's artistic sensibility.

Bendixen, Alfred. "Cable's *The Grandissimes:* A Literary Pioneer Confronts The Southern Tradition." *Southern Quarterly*, 18 (1980), 23–33.

In refusing to follow the conventions of the earlier plantation literature, Cable pioneered writing committed to a complex probing of Southern moral issues of both the past and present. Among the modern aspects of *G* are its treatment of the racial issue, its willingness to expose the violence and injustice of Southern life, its insistence that the lesson to be learned from the past is the need to adapt, the intense self-examination some of its characters undergo, its persistent questioning and its rich symbolism in characters' names.

Berkove, Lawrence I. "The Free Man of Color in *The Grandissimes* and Works by Harris and Mark Twain." *Southern Quarterly*, 18 (1980), 60–73.

Cable's use of the "free man of color" motif contrasts with the same motif in the 1880's fiction of Harris and Twain. In each case, the irony between the free man's legal designation and his actual freedom under the existing laws and social conventions is used to dramatize the violation of the Negroes' human rights.

Boyesen, Hjalmar H. "Cable's *Grandissimes.*" *Scribner's Monthly Magazine*, 20 (November 1880), pp. 159–61. Rpt. in Turner, *Critical Essays*, pp. 10–12.

G has "the beautiful spontaneity of an improvisation; although it is obviously the product of years of consideration." Boyesen suspects that Cable is attempting to teach some fundamental lessons of society and government to his fellow Southerners, although he ostensibly is the dispassionate historian. The influence of Frowenfeld, the central motif, is "unduly passive"; it is his lifestyle rather than his deeds which exalts the lives of those he meets. The final chapters drag, since the denouement after Chapter 43 becomes a foregone conclusion.

"Briefs on New Books." *Dial*, 1 (October 1880), pp. 115–16.

The institution of slavery and the spirit of caste among the Creoles play an important but unhackneyed part in this "first American novel of the year." The story is "striking" in originality and "dramatic" in effect, and some of the characterizations, such as Frowenfeld and the Creole ladies, are "wonderfully successful."

Brown, Sterling A. *The Negro in American Fiction*. Washington, D.C.: The Associates in Negro Folk Education, 1937, pp. 64–67.

The background of slavery in G is well defined, and the Negro characterizations are far more convincing than the abolitionist victims. Palmyre is one of the best characterized octoroons in fiction. Cable's fiction shows his full acquaintance with Southern life and language.

Brownell, W. C. "Cable's *The Grandissimes.*" *Nation*, 31 (December 9, 1880), pp. 415–16. Rpt. in Turner, *Critical Essays*, pp. 17–21.

The reader's first impression of G is that Cable is overturning new literary ground instead of breaking it. Brownell points out the serialization fault of ending each chapter on a note of suspense. Reading the entire work might clear up genealogical problems for the reader, but it becomes apparent that the genealogy is too beautifully done. Cable is at times rhetorically over-refined; everything is finally cleared up, but the uncertainty is annoying. Cable's chief fault in G is his romanticizing, since the best "modern" novels are studies of the subtlety of character.

Bullock, Penelope. "The Mulatto in American Fiction." *Phylon*, 6 (1945), 78–82.

Brief mention of G in this short, general study of the mulatto in American fiction. Cable's portraits are "sympathetic" and realistic, and his characters are three-dimensional. The portrayal of mulattoes by Cable and Charles Chesnutt are the "outstanding delineations of this character in nineteenth-century American fiction."

Butcher, Philip. "Cable to Boyesen on *The Grandissimes*," *American Literature* 40 (1968), 391–4.

The history of the correspondence of Cable and Boyesen is explained in this prefatory note to a previously unpublished letter from Cable to Boyesen on December 28, 1878. The letter expresses Cable's hopes for the literary and moral success of G, and also makes passing reference to the yellow fever epidemic then raging in New Orleans.

Butcher, Philip. "Impassioned Advocate." In his *George Washington Cable*. New York: Twayne Publishers, 1962, pp. 46–56.

Cable had great difficulties in creating a fictionally convincing hero or heroine, regardless of the praise of Barrie and Howells. The plot is always melodramatic, stereotypical, and superficially exotic, which reflects the author's romantic side. Yet ultimately G is a "penetrating study of a society torn by conflicting cultural traditions." The two heroes symbolize the contrasting civilizations in 1803 Louisiana. Frowenfeld is both a conscious and unconscious personification of changes in Cable's attitudes.

Campbell, Michael L. "The Negro in Cable's *The Grandissimes*." *Mississippi Quarterly*, 26 (1974), 43–54.

Campbell notes an ambivalence in Cable's attitude toward the blacks of G. Though pitying them for their sufferings, Cable was fascinated by and fearful of their suppressed violence and sexuality. Campbell refutes the idea that Cable's blacks are conventional stereotypes and emphasizes their role in depicting the complexities of black-white relations. By making his four black characters function organically in the plot and by revealing the naivete of Frowenfeld's demands for immediate reform, Cable is able to give an authentic and balanced treatment of a race problem.

Chase, Richard. "Cable and His *Grandissimes*." *Kenyon Review*, 18 (Summer 1956), 373–83. Rpt. in *The American Novel and Its Tradition*. Garden City, N. Y.: Doubleday, 1957, pp. 167–76.

G is Cable's first full expression of his position as an "ex-Confederate," someone who has divorced himself from the sectionalism of the South and taken up instead the nationalist view of politics and literature. Chase compares G, as a novel of manners, to a A *Hazard of New Fortunes*, *The Princess Cassamassima*, and the works of Twain. Although G lacks an epistemological symbolism and should not be regarded as "symbolic," the light-dark treatment and the ambiguity of reality are highly effective.

Clark, William Bedford. "Cable and the Theme of Miscegenation in *Old Creole Days and The Grandissimes*." *Mississippi Quarterly*, 30 (1977), 597–609.

The theme of miscegenation became Cable's vehicle for the larger themes of racial oppression and the transmission of guilt from one generation to another. Cable adopted the abolitionist image of the South as "a great brothel" for his own fiction. In G miscegenation became the emblem for the South's inheritance of racial wrongs.

Clark, William Bedford. "Humor in Cable's *The Grandissimes*." *Southern Quarterly*, 18 (1980), 51–9.

The humor of G, while tied to the tradition of local color and the comedy of manners, also provides a necessary distance from the brutality and ugliness of the theme of social injustice. The very structure of the novel follows a conventionally "comic" pattern in which lovers overcome familial and social obstacles to their wedding. Often, Cable's humor is juxtaposed against a very serious scene, as when Agricola in the prelude to his fatal encounter with Honoré f. m. c. makes himself unintentionally laughable.

Cleman, John. "The Art of Local Color in George W. Cable's *The Grandissimes*." *American Literature*, 47 (1975), 396–410.

Taking issue with critics who have sought to rescue G from the label of "mere" local color, Cleman argues that the art of color in G is subtle, complex, and the novel is great because of the color rather than in spite of it. The sense of mystery and ambiguity, so crucial to G, is dramatically and significantly deepened through the use of the natural environment, critical to "the intimations of violence" at the novel's heart. Parallels between the development of the Creole society and the development of the physical environment are thematically critical.

Cowie, Alexander. "Local-Color, Frontier and Regional Fiction: George Washington Cable (1844–1925)." In *The Rise of the American Novel*. New York: American Book Co., 1948, pp. 556–67.

Cowie notes the problem with labelling G as either romantic or realistic. Atmosphere finally characterizes the novel. Cable saw clearly the problems facing the races in New Orleans, but "as novelist he refuses to lease his story for purposes of propaganda. . . ." The author is interested more in place and period than in the problem of race. In his style, Cable does not aim at "brilliance but at intimacy."

G, though Cable's best book, demonstrates his abilities and faults: clumsy plot management, superb restitution in episode and description, and fine word sense.

Eaton, Richard Bozman. "George W. Cable and the Historical Romance." *Southern Literary Journal*, 8 (1975), 82–94.

Although *G* reflects the literary trend toward realism of its own time, Cable was simultaneously responding to the artistic requirements of another literary tradition—the historical romance. Eaton contends that the structural difficulties in *G* are the result of Cable's attempt to fuse the two distinct genres. *G* is analyzed along the plot lines of Scott's historical novels, with Frowenfeld as the outsider caught up in the surge of events. However, it is wrong to expect of *G* the bildungsroman pattern in which Frowenfeld discovers the world around him and either accepts or rejects its viewpoint. His remoteness is necessary for the novel's perspective.

Egan, Joseph J. "Lions Rampant: Agricola Fusilier and Bras-Coupé as Antithetical Doubles in *The Grandissimes*." *Southern Quarterly*, 18 (1980), 74–80.

Agricola Fusilier and Bras-Coupé are compared as antithetical doubles or alter-egos. Both are aristocrats in their respective worlds, and both are described through leonine metaphors. Racial hostility and a penchant for violence destroy both. The ultimate struggle between white and black is symbolized in the final clash between Agricola Fusilier and Bras-Coupé. For his sin, the refusal to recognize the basic humanity and brotherhood of all men, Agricola is destroyed by his "shadow."

Ekstrom, Kjell. "Cable's *Grandissimes* and the Creoles." *Studia Neophilologica*, 21 (Autumn 1949), 190–94.

Ekstrom quotes from two articles first printed in *The Critic* after the publication of *G*, and concludes from the evidence that "we have grounds in suspecting that Cable drew his Creole characters in *G* from life and that this was the main cause of the furious Creole reaction against this book." Ekstrom's article consists primarily of quotations from the *Critic* articles and a letter to the editor by Cable to *The Critic*.

Ekstrom, Kjell. *George Washington Cable: A Study of His Early Life and Work*. Uppsala: A-V. Lundequistska Bokhandeln and Cambridge, Mass.: Harvard University Press, 1950.

G is examined in chapters dealing with various works by Cable. Chapter V discusses the dating of sections of the novel in relation to internal evidence and the letters of Cable and Boyesen and the editing done by Scribner's. Chapter IX deals with possible literary influences on *G*, while Chapter X discusses possible non-literary sources. In Chapter XI Ekstrom compares the author's treatment of the Creoles in *G* to that in *Old Creole Days, Madame Delphine,* and *Dr. Sevier.*

Evans, William. "French-English Literary Dialect in *The Grandissimes." American Speech,* 46, Nos. 3–4 (Fall–Winter 1971), 210–22.

Evans, a linguist, discusses Cable's handling of the Creole dialect in *G.* Cable's French-English dialect in this novel functions effectively in linking like characters, in differentiating contrasting characters, and in distinguishing different moods in a single character.

Hamilton, Drayton, and W. Kenneth Holditch. "*The Grandissimes* and the French Quarter." *Southern Quarterly,* 18 (1980), 34–50.

Ten scenes from the French Quarter associated with *G* are presented in this photographic essay. The text accompanying the photographs offers historical information on the locations as well as comment on Cable's use of them.

Hearn, Lafcadio. "*The Grandissimes.*" New Orleans *Item,* September 27, 1880. Rpt. in Turner, *Critical Essays,* pp. 8–9.

Hearn's review does not attempt to tell the public what *G* is, but rather "to express in a few words the particular impression" which, as art, it produces on the reader. *G* is "the most remarkable work of fiction ever created in the South." The descriptive passages give one the feeling of a New Orleans familiar yet unknown. Cable's power of concentrated description is especially striking. The "merit of the romance" is not damaged by Cable's "peculiar views," but it is questionable whether such a character as Honoré Grandissime ever lived.

Howell, Elmo. "George Washington Cable's Creoles: Art and Reform in *The Grandissimes.*" *Mississippi Quarterly,* 26 (1972–73), 43–53.

Cable's art in this novel is marred by his aloofness. Though he observes and records the rich panorama of Louisiana and revels in the natural scene, he feels none of the pathos of the Creole's situation in the early nineteenth century nor of the white Southerner's predicament after 1865. His dialect passages fail because they convey the author's contempt.

Howells, William Dean. "Mr. G. W. Cable's Aurora and Clotilde Nancanou." In *Heroines of Fiction.* 2 Volumes. New York: Harper and Brothers, 1901; V. II, pp. 234–44. Rpt. in Turner, *Critical Essays,* pp. 123–25.

A florid essay by Howells on Cable's heroines. "The heroines of Mr. Cable's admirable novel, *The Grandissimes,* could be proved, at least to the satisfaction of their present elderly adorer, easily first among the imaginary ladies with whose sweetness novelists have enriched and enlarged our acquaintance. . . ." The blend of romance and reality do no harm to each other. Howells is convinced of the "positive exellence" of G. Much of this essay consists of passages from the novel.

Johnson, Robert Underwood. "George Washington Cable." In *Commemorative Tributes to Cable, . . . Sargent, . . . Pennell*. New York: American Academy of Arts and Letters, Publication No. 57, 1927, pp. 1–6. Rpt. in *Commemorative Tributes of the American Academy of Arts and Letters*. New York: American Academy of Arts and Letters, 1942, pp. 178–80.

Cable, with the exception of Poe and Hawthorne, is the greatest figure in American fiction. Historical background in G is lightly touched in, never intrusive. Cable is never commonplace in his style. G is "not only the greatest American novel to date[1908] but it stands in the front rank of the fiction of the world."

[King, Grace.] "A Southern Woman's Views of Mr. Cable's 'Grandissimes'." *Dial*, 1 (March 1881), p. 240.

Cable's treatment of Creole life is a "travesty," "as unreal as Chatterton's forgeries, and without his genius." The dialect is such as was never heard nor spoken in Louisiana. Clemence's murder is "dramatic and full of weird effects but it is a funny picture." Cable's book lacks the artistic merit of Tourgee's "Fool's Errand." King is "amazed" that Northern readers would believe that such people as the Grandissimes and Nancanous lived in Louisiana.

LeBreton, Dagmar Renshaw. *Chahta-Ima: The Life of Adrien-Emmanuel Rouquette*. Baton Rouge: Louisiana State University Press, 1947, pp. 319–23, et passim.

A study of the Rouquette papers offers no explanation as to the true authorship of *Aboo and Caboo*. The pamphlet is unworthy of Rouquette, although the Creoles had a just grievance against Cable for G.

Martin, Jay. *Harvests of Change: American Literature, 1865–1914*. Englewood Cliffs, NJ.: Prentice-Hall, 1967, pp. 100–05, et passim.

Cable is praised for refusing to seek refuge in a lost romantic past and for projecting its contradictions, frustrations, and the responsibility for finding solutions to its problems into the present. Analyzed from two perspectives, G is first a novel of unmasking, in which the main thematic thread is the unmasking by historical change of the vain attempt to preserve the past. Second, it is, as Boyesen has said, a kulturroman—a novel in which the struggling forces of opposing civilizations are delineated.

Mehta, R. N. "Cable's Handling of the Political Theme in *The Grandissimes*." in Naik, M. K., S. K. Desai, and S. Mokashi-Punekar, eds.

Indian Studies in American Fiction. Dharwar: Karnatak University; Delhi: Macmillan India, 1974, pp. 96–107.

G is a remarkable book principally on account of its bold and resolute handling of political and cultural themes. Mehta discusses Chase's comparison of G and James' *Princess Cassamassima*, finally disagreeing concerning Cable's parochialism. Cable's handling of general political ideas and issues is "confident, clear-eyed, even audacious," and continually related to political affairs of his own time. However, the stimulating discussions of political issues by themselves cannot account for the strength of G as a political novel.

Morse, James Herbert. "The Native Element in American Fiction, Since the War." *Century Magazine*, 26 (July 1883), pp. 368. Rpt. in Turner, *Critical Essays*, pp. 51–2.

The Creole element in G is delicate, poetic, and imaginative to a high degree. Cable was strong in creating a Creole aura, equal to Hawthorne's Puritan communities. The finest part of the artist's work is in the nice shading of character between Aurora and Clotilde. The dialect is also excellent. Cable's work is compared favorably to Eggleston's.

Pattee, Fred L. *A History of American Literature Since 1870*. New York: Century Company, 1915, pp. 246–53. Rpt. in Turner, *Critical Essays*, pp. 138–43.

Pattee feels that G is "a gallery rather than a single work of art," primarily because the "magnificent theme of the romance is not worked out." The novel is a rich mass of well-constructed scenes which "in a vague way" center around the story of Bras-Coupé. The theme is romantic rather than realistic throughout, the removal by innocent lovers of the curse of a dying man—"*The House of the Seven Gables* transferred to the barbarous swamps of the Atchafalaya."

Perret, J. John. "The Ethnic and Religious Prejudices of G. W. Cable." *Louisiana Studies*, 11 (Summer 1972), 263–73.

The dichotomy of Cable's ethnic and religious attitudes as exemplified in *Old Creole Days, Bonaventure*, and G is discussed. Cable was ostracized in New Orleans because of his insistence upon pleading the Negro cause, yet he could and did display "typically Southern WASP reactions." Perret argues that Cable's anti-Catholic bias was based on an ignorance of Catholic practices.

Quinn, Arthur H. *American Fiction*. New York: D. Appleton-Century-Crofts, 1936, p. 346.

G reveals Cable's strengths and weaknesses. The plot is involved to the extent that it creates confusion. The novel is loaded with unnecessary detail. The characters are realistic, however.

Review of *The Grandissimes*. *Atlantic Monthly*, 46 (December 1880), pp. 829–31. Rpt. in Turner, *Critical Essays*, pp. 13–15.

The internal evidence of conscientious labor is unmistakable. As a historical composition, G is frank and natural. Cable has not simply taken a picturesque theme and treated it truly and freshly; he has a "profound sense of the larger laws of history underlying the change" in the scenes. Frowenfeld serves as chorus, asking questions and bringing out prior conditions. His importance to the story is out of proportion to his value as one of the dramatis personae. The defects of the book may be traced to the struggle after adequate expression of commanding conception. The chronology is confusing, and the number of details detract from the interest.

Review of *The Grandissimes*. *Critic*, New Series, 31 (March 1899), p. 252.

G suffers because the problem is more absorbing than the people. The novel has many of the alluring qualities of Cable's short stories, but the reader feels that the author had studied the political and social aspects of his milieu to the extent that he is "possessed by the result of his study rather than by the personality of his creations." There is so much atmosphere, and the quality is so suave, that one may read G happily for the story's sake.

Review of *The Grandissimes*. *Harper's Magazine*, 62 (December 1880), p. 153. Rpt. in Turner, *Critical Essays*, p. 16.

G is a "spirited reproduction of the manners, customs, social life, and institutions" of early New Orleans. The narrative brings out in strong relief the characteristic traits of the Creoles, and in particular the exclusiveness and social grouping of the society. The action of the story generally is spirited, but its interest is diluted and its movement retarded by the undue space allotted to the reproduction of the peculiarities of intonation and dialect.

Review of *The Grandissimes*. *Literary World*, 11 (October 9, 1880), p. 347.

A short review of G. The "too-muchness" of the book is its main fault. "One gets tired of the indefinite extension of even such talented work." Cable has strong insight which cuts through the platitudes of the average Southern writing. However, G is a "first-rate literary performance," touched by few American novels in artistic strength, variety, and harmony.

Richardson, Thomas J. "Introduction: Honoré Grandissime's Southern Dilemma." *Southern Quarterly*, 18 (1980), 1–12.

In his introduction to a collection of essays marking the centennial of

G, Richardson offers a synopsis of the novel and then defines Honoré Grandissime's essential dilemma as the tension created between his attraction to the Creole world and those forces separating him from that world. The Creole world is associated with transience, mutability, and self-destructive pride. Not unlike his hero, Cable was caught between his desire to preserve the past and his desire to redeem the present. The great strength of *G*, Richardson suggests, rests in the momentary balance that Cable achieved between these tensions.

Ringe, Donald A. "The 'Double Center': Character and Meaning in Cable's Early Novels." *Studies in the Novel*, 5 (1973), 52–62.

G and *Dr. Sevier* are architecturally similar in focusing on a "double center" with emphases on shifting between a pair of characters. To seek a single spokesman for Cable in either novel is a critical error because the theme can emerge only through the interaction of the two main characters. In *G*, the interacting pair is Frowenfeld and Honoré Grandissime. To have made any single character spokesman would have over-simplified the social context and melodramatically divided the characters into heroes and villains.

Ringe, Donald A. "Narrative Voice in Cable's *The Grandissimes*." *Southern Quarterly*, 18 (1980), 13–22.

The narrative voice of *G*, an individual voice which assumes a personality of its own, gently leads the reader through the local color, the historical romance and the intricacies of Creole society. It locates the reader in time and space, lays the groundwork for the powerful themes emerging at the end of the novel, and helps control the reader's response to those themes. Most important, however, it will not let the reader escape the implication that what was true for the past is true for the present.

Rouquette, Adrian. *Critical Dialogue between Aboo and Caboo on a New Book; or, A Grandissimes Ascension.* New Orleans: Great Publishing House of Sam Slick Allspice, 1880.

A short (24pp.) virulent attack on Cable and *G* written in the form of a dialogue between two Creoles who meet in a swamp. Cable, the "Northern press," and "Charlemagne Scribner" all come under attack. *G*, rather than having any historical basis, is "the finical refinement of disguised puritanism, assuming the fanatical mission of radical reform and universal enlightenment." This pamphlet is more invective than rational complaint against the book. Cable is referred to as a possible "opium eater," since only through the medium of the drug could he have written a book reflective of his "deep-rooted guilt." The speakers claim that Cable has altered the facts—dates, names, places —and that they, rather than he, know the realistic Creole community.

Rubin, Louis D., Jr. "The Division of the Heart: Cable's *The Grandis-simes.*" *Southern Literary Journal*, 1 (1969), 27–47.

Rubin concludes that *G* is a deeply flawed work because of Cable's failure to reconcile the divisions of his artistic heart—i.e., his impulses as a social critic outraged at the injustice in the treatment of the Negro with his impulses as an artist who admired the distinction and distinctiveness of Creole society. An ambivalence in Cable's treat-ment of the Creoles flaws the novel: on the one hand he presents their negative qualities, and on the other he allows his spokesman Frowen-feld to become part of Creole society by marrying Clotilde. Rubin analyzes Agricola Fusilier as a symbol of the South and Frowenfeld as a spokesman for Cable.

Rubin, Louis D., Jr. "*The Grandissimes.*" In his *George W. Cable: The Life and Times of a Southern Heretic.* Pegasus American Authors Series. New York: Western Publishing Company, 1969, pp. 77–96.

Rubin claims that *G* is the first "modern" Southern novel, in the sense that it has been characterized by an uncompromising attempt to deal honestly with the complexity of Southern racial experience. *G* opened the path for the Southern novelists of the twentieth century to deal openly and honestly with this problem. The most striking feature of the novel is its rich social texture, akin to the Hawthornian dichotomy of Novel versus Romance. Although Cable emotes his political theories and solutions through and with Frowenfeld (as opposed to having his opinions become those *of* Frowenfeld), the way in which the outsider might respond to the vagaries of Creole civilization is presented somewhat weakly through the lifeless characterization of Frowenfeld.

Skaggs, Merrill M. "The Creole." In *The Folk of Southern Fiction.* Athens: University of Georgia Press, 1972, pp. 154–88.

Honoré Grandissime's romantic gesture (attempting to restore the lost fortune) better suits Cable's morality than the facts of the case. As a rule, however, Cable disapproved of the length to which a Creole would go to protect relatives. The author ridicules the Creole distinction between African and Indian blood in the Creoles and their pretensions to gentility. One of the greatest "evils" of this pretension is the Creole's contempt for honest labor. The novel makes it clear, however, that the pretensions are not limited to the Grandissime family.

Starke, Catherine Juanita. *Black Portraiture in American Fiction: Stock Characters, Archetypes, and Individuals.* New York: Basic Books, 1971. pp. 137–40.

In an analysis of black archetypes, Daggoo in *Moby Dick* and Bras-Coupé in *G* are contrasted as examples of the primitive. Bras-Coupé has a symbolic meaning, but his African name, Mioko-Koanga, is as foreign-sounding as Daggoo. Starke suggests that Cable's character is not as essential to him in *G* as Daggoo is to Melville in *Moby Dick*.

Stephens, R.O. "Cable's *The Grandissimes* and the Comedy of Manners." *American Literature*, 51 (1980), 507–19.

Stephens asserts that Cable's emphasis in *G* is on the Creole world, not on the clash between Creole and American civilizations. Pointing to Cable's statement of purposes in writing *G*, a statement which appeared in "Afterthoughts of a Story-Teller," Stephens concludes that Cable's purpose parallels the aim of the comedy of manners genre. In true comic tradition, the marriages of Honoré and Frowenfeld institute new reconciliations as the two heroes become fully incorporated into society. True also to the comic vision, Aurora refuses to accept Honoré on the basis of a parental promise and insists that his choice be personally and freely made.

Tinker, Edward Larocque. "Cable and the Creoles." *American Literature*, 5 (January 1934), 313–26.

Tinker points out that in *G* the reader sees the first indications that the propagandist was beginning to "strangle" the creative artist. Although this article is relatively short, it contains much interesting information, such as a list of editorials written by Hearn in praise of *G* and a possibly apocryphal story concerning James Barrie and a delegation of New Orleans ladies.

Turner, Arlin. *George W. Cable, A Biography*. Durham, N.C.: Duke University press, 1956, pp. 89–104.

This chapter in Turner's biography of Cable focuses particularly upon source material for *G*, the problems incurred during printing and editorial work, and the contemporary response by major and minor critics. Turner notes Cable's slow admittance of models for his main characters and comments briefly on the criticism of Howells and Johnson. The section dealing with the editorial work of Russell, Herrick, Johnson, Gilder, and Cable contains a number of comments written by the editors on the reverse of the manuscript sheets. Turner claims that more than one scene is saved from melodrama only by the firm hold the characters maintain on the action.

Turner, Arlin. *George W. Cable* (Southern Writers Series No. 1). Austin: Steck-Vaughn, 1969, pp. 8–12.

The general plot of G depicts two white civilizations struggling for dominance, while a third, subservient group seems to have the crucial role in shaping the future. Although the dialect and character relations might confuse the reader, he will sense the profusion of life and the intricacy of the world it creates. This section contains a summary of the editorial work of Cable, Johnson, Herrick, and Russell.

Wilson, Edmund. "The Ordeal of George Washington Cable." *New Yorker*, 33 (November 9, 1957), 180–228. Rpt. in *Patriotic Gore: Studies in the Literature of the American Civil War*. New York: Oxford University Press, 1962, pp. 548–87.

Essay-review of Arlin Turner's *George W. Cable*. Wilson notes the Southern literary tradition, beginning with Stowe and Boucicault, which deals with miscegenation, but adds that he does not believe Faulkner to have been influenced by Cable, though they have similar methodologies. The Victorian sensibility is effective in G, underlining the problem of the proximity of the races. The Bras-Coupé episode was probably influenced by the writings of Turgenev, whom Cable read in the Russian in 1874 while revising the novel. Wilson concludes that G is Cable's best book, and that the recent studies by Arvin and Chase are better than any studies done by Cable's contemporaries.

Notes on Contributors

ANTHONY J. ADAM is a doctoral student in English at Louisiana State University. He recently completed requirements for the M.A. in English at the University of Southern Mississippi.

ALFRED BENDIXEN is an assistant professor of English at Barnard College. His previous publications on Southern literature include an article on George W. Cable for *Louisiana Studies*.

LAWRENCE I. BERKOVE is a professor of English and American literature at the University of Michigan-Dearborn, and Director of the American Studies Program. He has authored a number of articles on nineteenth century American literature and has recently published *Skepticism and Dissent*, an edition of Ambrose Bierce's journalism from 1898–1901.

WILLIAM BEDFORD CLARK, a professor of English at Texas A & M University, has published on a wide range of topics in American literature. He is presently editing a volume on Robert Penn Warren for the G. K. Hall Essays in American Literature series.

JOSEPH J. EGAN is professor of English at Slippery Rock State College. His recent publications have appeared in *English Language Notes, Modern Fiction Studies,* and the *Colby Library Quarterly.*

DRAYTON HAMILTON, a native of Alabama, currently resides in New Orleans. He is working on a doctorate in philosophy at Johns Hopkins University.

W. KENNETH HOLDITCH, a poet and short story writer, is the book reviewer for the New Orleans *States-Item* and a professor of English at the University of New Orleans.

SARA McCASLIN is a graduate student in English at the University of Southern Mississippi.

DONALD A. RINGE, currently University Research Professor at the University of Kentucky, is the author of three books and numerous articles on nineteenth century American literature.

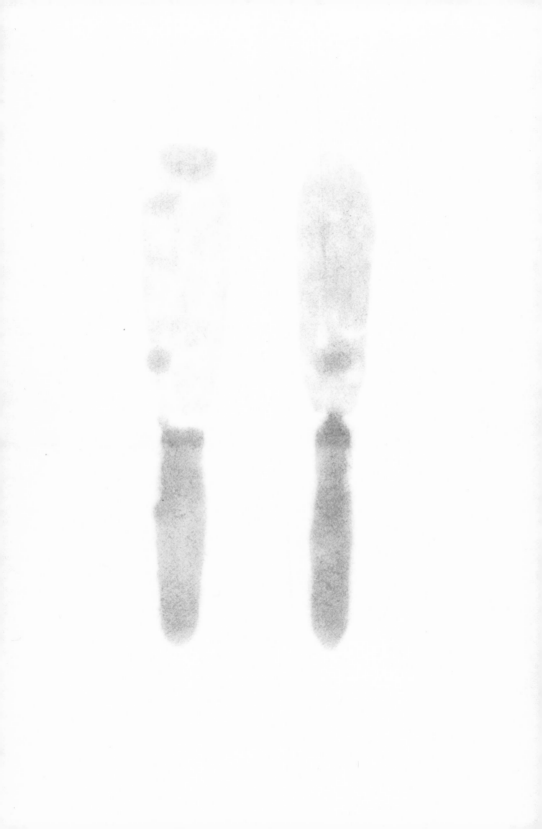